AF352691

ON SLAVERY AND THE SLAVE TRADE

EARLY MODERN
CATHOLIC SOURCES

Volume 8

LUIS DE MOLINA, SJ

ON SLAVERY AND THE SLAVE TRADE

DE IUSTITIA ET IURE, BOOK 1,
TREATISE 2, DISPUTATIONS 32–40

Translated by DANIEL SCHWARTZ
and JÖRG TELLKAMP

THE CATHOLIC UNIVERSITY
OF AMERICA PRESS
Washington, D.C.

Cataloging-in-Publication Data available

from the Library of Congress

ISBN: 978-0-8132-3749-7

eISBN: 978-0-8132-3750-3

Daniel Schwartz dedicates this book

to his children Alma and Yonathan

and Jörg Tellkamp to his,

Valentina and Lukas.

CONTENTS

ACKNOWLEDGMENTS

This project has been in the making for several years. Jörg would like to thank Thomas Duve at the Max-Planck Institute for Legal History and Legal Theory in Frankfurt. A four-month research grant there allowed him to work not only on the manuscript but also to meet colleagues working on the intersection of the history of legal thought, ethics, and slavery.

Anne-Charlotte Martineau and Rômulo Ehalt, whom we met at events in Frankfurt, Louvain-la-Neuve, and Paris, generously shared their insights and expertise with us. We would also like to thank John Thornton for his guidance on all matters related to African history and the Atlantic slave trade. Claude Stuczynski shared his expert knowledge of Portuguese *conversos*. Matthias Lutz-Bachmann, Matthias Kaufmann, Wim Decock, Giuseppe Marcocci, Catherine Sims, and Jacob Schmutz provided helpful advice and support at different stages of the process that ultimately led to this book.

Translating Molina was not an easy task. We are thankful to Jenni Glaser whose preliminary translations of some of the disputations provided a valuable foundation for our work. Elizabeth Miles did an outstanding job editing, correcting, and improving the final text.

We would like to express our gratitude to Ulrich L. Lehner and Trent Pomplun, the editors of the Early Modern Catholic Sources series, who saw promise in our project. We also extend our thanks to Michele Callaghan at the Catholic University of America Press for her meticulous copy editing of the manuscript, and to John Martino who oversaw the editorial work with a sure hand.

ABBREVIATIONS AND COMMON FOREIGN TERMS

a. article

c. chapter

CC-COGD Corpus Christianorum Conciliorum Oecumenicorum Generaliumque Decreta

Cod. *Codex iustinianus*

col. column

coll. *collatio*

comm. commentary

d. distinction

D. *Decretum Magistri Gratiani*

DIEI *De iustitia et iure*

dig. *digressio*

Dig. *Digestum* in *Corpus Iuris Civilis*

dub. doubt

fol. folio

ley law

lib. book

n. paragraph number

Pars part

Partida one of the *Siete Partidas*

prol. prologue

q. question

resol. solution

sect. section

tit. title

tract. treatise

VI *Liber sextus decretalium*

X *Liber extravagantium decretalium* (*Liber extra*)

ON SLAVERY AND
THE SLAVE TRADE

Introduction

In 1443, the explorer Nuno Tristão returned to Portugal from the Bay of Arguin, in present-day Mauritania, with fourteen enslaved persons on board. One year later, when Lançarote de Freitas landed 235 captured Africans in Lagos, Portugal, the mass slave trade across the Atlantic had officially begun. The slavery business was booming during the time the Spanish theologian Luis de Molina lived in Portugal, from 1568 to 1600.[1] Molina was uniquely placed to subject the slave trade to a thorough moral and legal examination. Indeed, he reports that he interviewed slave merchants to get the facts right for what he regarded as a "diligent investigation" on the matter of slavery.[2] His inquiries should not have been difficult to make, since the São Roque Professed House,

---

1. See Frank B. Costello, *The Political Philosophy of Luis de Molina, SJ (1535–1600)* (Rome/Spokane: Institutum historicum Societatis Iesu, 1974), 3–22.

2. Luis de Molina, *De iustitia et iure*, tract. II, d. 35, n. 16, which is on pp. 92–93 in this translation (hereafter *DIEI*). For the present translation, we used the Latin version in the bilingual Latin-German edition of *De iustitia et iure: Über die Gerechtigkeit und Recht*, ed. Matthias Kaufmann and Danaë Simmermacher and trans. Alexander Loose, vol. 2 (Stuttgart/Bad Cannstatt: Frommann-Holzboog, 2019), 572–786. The text contained in those volumes is based on the *editio princeps* of Cuenca 1593, yet it includes a series of corrections. Unless otherwise noted, the citations from Molina refer to that edition.

References to the text translated provide treatise number, disputation, and paragraph number as per the Latin text in the Latin-German translation *Über die Gerechtigkeit und Recht*. References for texts from volumes 1 and 2 of *DIEI* provide treatise number, disputation, column number, and letters referring to text sections as per the original editions of Cuenca 1593 by Juan Masselini and 1598 by Miguel Serrano de Vargas. References to texts from volume 5 of *DIEI* provide treatise, disputation, and paragraph number as per the edition of Sessa, Venice 1611.

where Molina lived during his Lisbon period, was just a ten-minute walk to the Casa dos Escravos, one of the places where African slaves were held before being sold.[3] In fact, at the time, between 10 and 16 percent of the population in Lisbon was made up of African slaves and there were many slave markets across the city.[4]

The moral and legal quandaries that arose from the slave trade had already been addressed before Molina. Yet Molina's effort stands out because his take on slavery is based on thoroughly developed theoretical foundations. He sees slavery as a legal, social, and economic phenomenon the analysis of which requires first clarifying fundamental concepts such as rights and ownership. If slavery constitutes some kind of ownership, it is necessary first to examine what it means to own a person and whether one human being can own another and in what way. In his magnum opus, *De iustitia et iure libri sex* (Six books on justice and rights), Molina devoted disputations 32–40 of the second treatise to the question of slavery (*servitus* or *mancipium*). In this book, we provide the first English translation of this important text.

Luis de Molina

Luis de Molina is considered to be, along with Francisco de Vitoria and Francisco Suárez, one of the most important representatives of late Scholasticism and of what is often called the School of Salamanca. Luis de Molina was born in Cuenca, Spain, in 1535 to Diego Orejón y Muela and Ana García de Molina.[5] He received his Latin education in his hometown. He went to study law in Salamanca for one year and then

3. See John K. Vogt, "The Lisbon Slave House and African Trade, 1486–1521," *Proceedings of the American Philosophical Society* 117 (1973): 1–16.

4. See A. J. R. Russell Wood, "Iberian Expansion and the Issue of Black Slavery: Changing Portuguese Attitudes, 1440–1770," *American Historical Review* 83, no. 1 (1978): 22.

5. This biographical sketch collates information from the following sources: Iohannes Rabeneck, "De vita et scriptis Ludovicis Molina," *Archivum Historicum Societatis Iesu* 19 (1950): 75–145; Luis de Molina, "Discurso Preliminar," in *Los seis libros de la justicia y el derecho*, trans., prologue, and notes by Manuel Fraga Iribarne (Madrid: Cosano, 1941), vol. 1, 18–33; and Raoul de Scorraille, *François Suárez de la Compagnie de Jésus* (Paris: Lethielleux, 1914), 398–405.

logic in Alcalá, where he joined the Company of Jesus in August 1553. By the end of that month, he matriculated as a student of arts in Coimbra, the most prestigious university in Portugal. He began theology courses after completing four years of arts and was ordained a priest in 1561 or 1562. That same year he moved to the University of Evora in southern Portugal to obtain his doctoral degree. It is there that he started his long teaching career, first teaching the arts course, then theology, and as of 1571 serving as chair of prima in theology, which was the most prestigious lecture in the morning hours.

Molina is reported to have had an unimpressive physical presence. Of small body frame, he was not particularly good looking and dressed poorly. He used to carry his papers in an old bag "as if they were rubbish to be thrown to the river,"[6] but his eloquence made listeners quickly overcome their first impressions. However, he was insecure about his Latin and was urged to get help to improve his style, which he did (though he feared that the imposition of a more stylish humanist Latin could distort the meaning of his theories).[7] He was not particularly modest about his own work, often extolling it in his letters.[8] From his extensive correspondence with Claudio Acquaviva, the general of the Jesuit order, we also learn that Molina often complained about some hostility from Portuguese fellow Jesuits, which he attributed to his being a foreigner, an attitude that apparently persisted even after living

6. De Scorraille, *François Suárez*, 399. We could not find these exact words in the works cited by de Scorraille: Alonso de Andrade, *Varones ilustres de la Compañia de Iesus* (Madrid: Fernández de Buendía, 1666), vol. 5, 790, the *Litterae Annuae Societatis Iesu, Anni MDC* (Antwerp: Nutio and Muerisio, 1618), 157, and Joseph Jouvency, *Historiæ Societatis Jesu pars quinta* (Rome: Plachi, 1710), 825–26. Andrade does point out that "El Padre Molina los miraba con tal desprecio que estudiaba y enseñaba en papeles viejos, cubiertas de cartas y pliegos quebrados, juzgando en mal gastado buen papel en su doctrina." (Father Molina treated his writings with such contempt that he studied and taught with old sheets of paper, letter envelopes, and broken folded pages, judging good paper to be badly used when used to write on it his own doctrine). Andrade, *La Compañia de Iesus*, 790.

7. Molina to Jesuit general Claudio Aquaviva, March 6, 1583, published in Friedrich Stegmüller, *Geschichte des Molinismus* (Münster: Aschendorff, 1935), 562, line 34; 566, lines 40–45.

8. Molina to Acquaviva, August 6, 1582, in Stegmüller, *Molinismus*, 552, lines 25–30.

thirty years in Portugal.[9] He ultimately felt that his contribution to the Jesuit province of Portugal was not sufficiently appreciated.[10] In 1585 or 1586, he moved to Lisbon to the Professed House of São Roque, where he worked on *De iustitia et iure*. He returned to Cuenca in 1591 and moved to Madrid in 1600 to teach at the Colegio Imperial, where he died on October 12 of that year.

Three of Molina's works were published during his lifetime: *De liberi arbitrii cum gratiae donis, divina praescientia, praedestinatione et reprobatione concordia* (1588), *Commentaria in Primam Divi Thomae Partem* (1592), and *De iustitia et iure libri sex* (1593–1600). A short treatise on faith was published posthumously.[11] He left many unpublished manuscripts, most of which are early drafts of his published work. The first draft of the discussion on slavery translated in this volume may have been completed in October 1586.[12] It is clear from internal evidence that the writing was not completed until at least 1586 because Molina mentions a deal between the Portuguese and the Zamorin of Calicut that was concluded that year.[13]

Molina on Slavery and Enslavement

It is important to keep in mind that the present text was not intended to be an independent treatise on slavery. Rather it has to be seen in the broader context of his legal magnum opus *De iustitia et iure*, which consisted of six volumes in total. Of the 760 disputations contained in the second treatise, it is only disputations 32 to 40 that deal with the problem of slavery. In the second treatise, Molina builds on the con-

9. Molina to Aquaviva, March 6, 1583, in Stegmüller, *Molinismus*, 562, lines 15, 34; 566, lines 40–45, and October 30, 1583, in Stegmüller, *Molinismus*, 580, line 22.

10. Molina to Acquaviva, October 30, 1583, in Stegmüller, *Molinismus*, 574, line 10; 578, lines 5–10.

11. J. A. Aldama, "Luis de Molina S.J. De spe: Comentario a la 2a2ae, 17–22," *Archivo Teológico Granadino* 1 (1938): 111–48.

12. This being the manuscript titled *Tractatus secundus. De iustitia commutativa circa bona corporis.* 1581. Stegmüller, *Molinismus*, 12*.

13. K. S. Mathew, "Calicut, the International Emporium of Maritime Trade and the Portuguese during the Sixteenth Century," *Proceedings of the Indian History Congress* 67 (2006–2007): 261.

ceptual framework that he had introduced in the first treatise regarding the notions of right (*ius*) and justice (*iustitia*). It is immediately clear that he draws heavily on the ancient and medieval legal tradition that is anchored in two main sources. One is the *Corpus iuris civilis*, commonly known as Roman Law. It had been formulated in various stages from the second to the sixth centuries AD, that is, from Gaius to Justinian. The second seminal legal text he draws on is that of Canon Law, the *Corpus iuris canonici*, at the center of which was a body of texts known as the *Decretum Gratiani*, authored by the jurist Gratian in the twelfth century. Molina, however, was keenly aware of several other sources, juridical and theological, such as the *Siete Partidas* of Alfonso X, and the so-called post-glossators, who were medieval jurists mostly from the fourteenth century who commented on the mentioned bodies of texts. Considering his awareness of the long-standing tradition and transmission of legal and theological knowledge, one might ask what Molina's contribution to that field was. A part of the answer to that question is precisely what this volume sets out to achieve in the specific case of slavery.

The first treatise of *De iustitia et iure* discusses what rights and justice are.[14] Molina assumes that there are two fundamental features a person must at least potentially have in order to have a right and to invoke justice: free will (*liberum arbitrium*) and rationality (*ratio*). Adding the further assumption, made in the *Institutes*, that all human beings are born free, one might say that any rights can belong only to rational and free agents and that justice can only be owed to them. Importantly for the discussion on slavery, Molina believes that those basic traits also apply to slaves, since they, too, are evidently human beings.

Generally speaking, one can say that Molina does not think of justice in exclusively legal terms but rather prefers to interpret it in an Aristotelian fashion, namely as a virtue that strives to give the citizens of the republic the proper guidelines for an adequate life in society that ideally should aim at the common good.[15] In this respect, the proper

---

14. See Jörg Tellkamp, "Rights and Dominium," in *A Companion to Luis de Molina*, ed. Matthias Kaufmann and Alexander Aichele (Leiden/Boston: Brill, 2014), 125–53.

15. Molina, *DIEI*, I.1.6.

function of justice is to establish equity (*aequum*) among agents within a polity, who acquire rights (*iura*) to the extent that they interact with others.[16] However, the term *right* is, as Molina puts it, equivocal—that is, it has various meanings that cannot necessarily be reduced to one another. Following a definition given by Isidore of Seville in his *Etymologies* (seventh century), Molina notes that right (*ius*) is so called because it is just (*iustum*).[17] That, by itself, is not yet explicative of what rights are, but it already hints at an essential tenet: the proper object of rights is justice and the goal of justice (and therefore of rights) is to create some form of equity. For this reason, Molina continues to explore the meaning of justice by using the canonical definition given at the beginning of the *Institutes*: it is "an unswerving and perpetual will to acknowledge all men's rights."[18]

The reference to the will is essential, for it establishes, in Molina's interpretation, a meaning of rights and justice as claims of and over something. The definition of a right as "a faculty or power, which man has with respect to something" highlights Molina's conviction that having rights usually is akin to having the power to express a claim over something.[19] A right can furthermore be merely natural (*ius naturale*) or it can be positive (*ius positivum*). In stressing the role of natural rights, Molina carefully introduces the notion of *dominium*, broadly standing for a wide range of ownership or property rights.

In his view, the division of things (*divisio rerum*) was a rational necessity once humankind fell from grace, because in the postlapsarian state people started quarreling about control over material things. Although by natural law everything was originally common and no private property existed, the change in human nature after the Fall made it necessary to introduce norms and rules that would stop people from

16. Molina, *DIEI*, I.1.11: "Alio modo sumitur iustitia, ut est particularis virtus in ordine ad alterum, cuius obiectum est iustum presse ac proprie sumptum, ut est idem, quod aequum, cuius oppositum est iniquum, quod iniuriam alterius comparatione involvit."

17. Molina, *DIEI*, I.2.1.

18. *Justinian's Institutes*, trans. and intro. Peter Birks and Grant McLeod (London: Duckworth, 2001), 37: "Iustitia est constans et perpetua voluntas ius suum cuique tribuens." Slightly altered translation.

19. Molina, *DIEI*, I.2.4.

harming each other as they attempted to impose their selfish desires on others. Among those "things" that fall under the general term of ownership are also persons, that is, slaves. Slavery, as Molina argues in accordance with the legal tradition, is the result of a common normative agreement of the peoples—the law of nations (*ius gentium*).

One of the main purposes of Molina's legal magnum opus is to introduce and establish the basic conceptual lexicon necessary for a correct analysis of rights in the public and in the private sphere. Rights are mostly relational in the sense that they refer to things that are the object of such a right. In other words, a right would be meaningless if it did not refer to something specific, be it material or immaterial. These rights are also transactional in the sense that, whenever a right is claimed by one person, its adequate enforcement tends to affect the situation of someone else. This is why, for Molina, commutative justice (or justice of exchanges) is a subdivision of justice that is central to a proper understanding of the nature of rights understood as claims. At the basis of commutative justice, we find the notion of ownership (*dominium*), which represents the most paradigmatic meaning of right, namely, the right over something. The owner of an object, say a book, can fundamentally lay a valid claim on it, that is, he can provide solid reasons why it belongs to him.

The main distinction between kinds of *dominia* is that between jurisdictional ownership (*dominium iurisdictionis*) as exercised by sovereigns and ownership qua property (*dominium proprietatis*) as enjoyed by private persons with respect to material or immaterial goods. For Molina the discussion of slavery belongs to the realm of private law, mostly because the ownership of one human being over another is in a way similar to the ownership over any other material object. Yet, at the same time, ownership of a human being, which is strictly speaking ownership of his freedom, has various features that set it apart in crucial ways from *dominium* of inanimate objects and nonhuman animals.

To see this, note first that, for ownership to be fully valid, there must be an ontological asymmetry between the object and the subject of *dominium*. For example, a human being can own a book because rationality and free will warrant that the subject can claim a right over this object, while the object cannot do the same vis à vis the subject because a book is not rational and free. This means that the property relation between subject and object presupposes a hierarchical order between subject and object.

At the beginning of the third treatise, Molina addresses the question of whether one human being can be the owner (*dominus*) of his or her life and body.[20] Natural law precludes such ownership, says Molina, since, in the whole of creation, only God can be *dominus* of the things that are beneath him, which obviously includes human beings, their lives, and their bodies.[21] All healthy adult human beings have rationality and free will and, given the lack of ontological inequality among human beings, no property over the lives and bodies of other humans can be admitted in that realm.

Molina also believes that it is against right reason to interfere with the lives or bodies of other people, since such an action would constitute an injustice toward them and toward God.[22] For example, harming or killing oneself or others without sufficient justification is a morally reprehensible offense.[23] Interfering with one's own body, such as in the case self-mutilation, or with that of others is justified only when it does not contradict right reason (*recta ratio*). Furthermore, such an action should not cause more harm than the harm it prevents, as in the case of amputating a gangrenous limb to save a person's life.

An immediate consequence of the lack of essential differences between human beings is Molina's rejection of the Aristotelian notion of natural slavery. In the sixteenth century, the rejection of natural slavery became official church doctrine when Pope Paul III, in his bull *Inter caetera* from 1537, declared that the Indigenous peoples of the Americas could not be enslaved. In disputation 32, Molina does give an account of the Aristotelian distinction, and he concedes that there may be natural differences among human beings, but he argues that these dif-

---

20. Molina, *DIEI*, III.1. (Venice: Sessa, 1611) vol. 4.

21. Molina, *DIEI*, III.1.2: "Homo non est dominus propriae vitae, ac membrorum, sicut est dominus pecuniae, et caeterorum bonorum externorum, quae ad ipsam spectant, ac possidet." Also n. 4: "Constitutus item est custos et administrator vitae ac membrorum."

22. Molina, *DIEI*, III.1.3.

23. Molina, *DIEI*, III.1.2: "Non minus eo praecepto [the fifth commandment] esse prohibitum occidere se ipsum, quam alium."

ferences cannot establish the subjection of one person to another, unless that person were to submit to it willingly.

If slavery is to be justified, it would have to be limited in a way that property over inanimate things is not. This means that human beings enjoy only a temporary permission to exercise some kind of possession of themselves and of others.[24] Full human ownership of another human being or of themselves is impossible from the point of view of divine law and because the natural basis for such ownership is absent.[25] For this reason, for Molina, the justification of slavery does not belong to natural law but rather to the sphere of municipal positive law and the law of nations (*ius gentium*).[26]

Molina's account of slavery constitutes a legal and moral reflection on a social and legal institution that has been seen—at least since the Quakers criticized it in 1688—as being obviously wrongful from a moral point of view.[27] Rather than rejecting the institution as such, Molina analyzes it in the light of how commerce and property rights were being articulated in the early modern Iberian Peninsula. He does so by bringing to the fore a set of normative principles that may strike us as uncomfortably "medieval" and yet, in some instances, as surprisingly modern.

Luis de Molina's analysis of the legal conditions and implications of slavery was not, of course, the first. As we have seen, it harks back to a long-standing tradition, mostly to Roman Law and the tradition of legal commentary in the Middle Ages, which sees it as mainly as a matter of contract law in which the slave's labor becomes a tradable object. To be a slave means roughly to lose all social freedoms and rights, which is

24. Molina, *DIEI*, III.1.3.

25. Molina, *DIEI*, III.1.3: "Ergo censendum est, non fecisse homines dominos ipsorum vitae, ut eam sibi eripere possent antequam per causas, iuxta sua divinae providentiae ordinem, ab eis eripere [. . .] quoniam neque lumen ipsum naturae, neque naturalis inclinatio tanta, quantam a homines habent, in seque ipsis experiuntur, ad propriae vitae conservationem, docent, cum illisve consentit, hominibus a natura ipsa, iureve naturali, esse concessum, posse sibi eripere propriam vitam; neque iure divino positivo reperitur id consecessum."

26. Molina, *DIEI*, I.4.8, 42 (Stuttgart-Bad Cannstatt : Frommann-Holzboog) : "Communiter dici consuevit, nempe de iure naturali fuisse omnia communia, iure vero gentium introductam factamque fuisse rerum divisionem."

27. See Brycchan Carey and Geoffrey Plank, "Introduction," in *Quakers and Abolition*, ed. Carey, Brycchan, and Plank (Urbana/Chicago/Springfield: University of Illinois Press, 2014), 3. We thank Anthony Pagden for pointing us to this precedent.

the consequence of having been transformed into an object over which someone exercises powers and rights.[28] As early as the time of Justinian's *Institutes*, it is acknowledged that slaves, as human beings, are not just any tradable object; they are special. There it says the following:

The reality of the human condition led the peoples of the world to introduce certain institutions. Wars broke out. People were captured and made slaves contrary to the law of nature. By the law of nature (*iure naturali*) all men were initially born free. Nearly all the contracts come from this law of all peoples—sale, hire, partnership, deposit, loan, and many others.[29]

This brief passage is already indicative of a salient aspect of trade, which, although mostly associated with the trade in inanimate objects, also includes the trade in living beings, namely, animals and human beings. Slaves, however, even though they are a tradable commodity, are seen as substantially different from other commodities. Unlike cattle or inanimate objects, slaves are human beings who are endowed with reason and natural freedom, the loss of which can only be the consequence of human institutions and forms of interaction introduced by the law of nations (*ius gentium*), such as commerce and war. In this respect, it is worth quoting at length the conceptual introduction of slavery in the context of private law or the law of persons (*ius personarum*) from the *Institutes*:

28. It might be relevant to note that the terms *servus*, *mancipium*, and *servitus*, that is, slave and slavery, share one common definition that consists in the loss of civil and social freedom. Although slavery is usually associated with the harsh realities of forced and unpaid labor, it also has to be taken into account that often slaves performed labors that competed with the labor of free people. The term *slave*, thus, covered a spectrum of degrees of subjection. Giuseppe Dari-Mattiacci and Guilherme de Oliviera, based on existing academic work, think that in Africa slave labor did not designate a rigid category. In some regions, such as West and Central-Western Africa, slavery complemented free labor from within communities and households. By contrast, in closed societies that ostracized enslaved communities, such as the antebellum South, slave labor was completely separated from the free labor market and would not compete with it. See Giuseppe Dari-Mattiacci and Guilherme de Oliveira, "Slavery versus Labor," *Review of Law & Economics* 17 (2021), 505. It seems clear that what Molina had in mind when discussing slavery was more likely the way the institution presented itself in African societies, rather than the shape it took in the American colonies—an economic exploitation in unskilled tasks, such as harvesting sugarcane.

29. *Justinian's Institutes*, 37.

The main classification in the law of persons is this: all men (*homines*) are either free or slaves. Liberty—the Latin *libertas* gives us *liberi*, free men—denotes a man's natural ability to do what he wants as long as the law or some other force does not prevent him. Slavery on the other hand is an institution of the law of all peoples; it makes a man the property (*dominium*) of another, contrary to the law of nature. Slaves, in Latin *servi*, are so called because it is the practice of army commanders to order captives to be sold and thus saved—"save" in Latin is *servare*—instead of killed. Another Latin word for slaves is *mancipia*, derived from the fact that they are captured by hand from the enemy, in Latin *manu capiuntur*. They are either born slaves or enslaved afterward. The offspring of slave women are born slaves. Enslavement can happen under the law of all peoples, by capture; or under the law of the state, as when a free man over twenty allows himself to be sold to share the price. The legal condition of all slaves is the same. Among free men there are many distinctions. Free men are either free-born or freed.[30]

Here, the *Institutes* anticipate what medieval legal literature considered the legitimate causes of loss of freedom: war, birth, self-sale, crime, deceitful self-sale, and ingratitude.[31] Although we discuss these causes below, it is important first to examine more closely the dichotomy between being free and being a slave, because at this point, we are faced with a paradox. If, as the *Institutes* state, "by the law of nature all men were initially born free" (I, 2), then the subjection to slavery must be the result of a departure from the original natural state, which came about when social life evolved after the fall from grace. Increasing social complexity, together with the desire for self-preservation both as a species and as individuals, as well as vices such as greed, made it necessary to establish norms that applied not only to individual human behavior (regulated by natural law) but also to the interactions between national communities or peoples. This was the law of nations or peoples (*ius gentium*).

While the *Corpus iuris civilis* already had a full-blown legal theory of slavery, it appears that this legalistic point of view was considered to be open to revision from a theological perspective. Even though legally protected from mistreatment, slaves were originally thought to have

---

30. *Justinian's Institutes*, 39.

31. Eike Hamann, *Die Begründung des Sklavenstatus bei den Postglossatoren: die Frage nach der Rezeption römischen Sklavenrechts* (Hamburg: Kovac, 2011), 185–205.

lost all civil rights, including the right to own property. However, the various Christian adaptations of the *Corpus iuris civilis* had to deal with the overarching project of the Christian faith, that is, the salvation of souls, which was absent in pre-Christian Roman times. This goal, made necessary by religious mandates, was not seen as inherently inconsistent with the coercive nature of slavery.[32] Yet it also helped to shift the focus from slavery as an instrument of mere exploitation to a form of subordination in which slaves were given certain enforceable rights by virtue of their humanity. As our translation shows, in disputation 38 Molina endorses the idea that slaves should not, and perhaps not even primarily, be seen simply as slaves but rather as humans in a condition of slavery. As human beings, they have, as already mentioned, certain characteristics, such as reason and free will, that enable them to exercise rights, that is, to articulate enforceable claims, not only in a moral sense but sometimes also in a legal sense. Among these rights we find the right to own property, to marry (marriage is a kind of contract that requires the free consent of the parties), and the right to care for spiritual needs.[33] In this sense, the owner of slaves and the slaves themselves could celebrate valid contracts as legal equals.[34]

Molina's treatise offers a rich, multifaceted analysis of the concept and the institution of slavery. His arguments regarding the just reasons for enslaving a person are equally intricate. The philosophical tradition based on Aristotle's *Politics* used to distinguish between natural and legal slavery. Natural slavery, on the one hand, was the result of natural differences that would make it almost necessary for some people to become slaves so that they may benefit from the relationship of subordination.[35] Legal slavery, on the other hand, was a consequence of human conventions, such as the enslavement of people captured in

---

32. Alice Rio, *Slavery after Rome, 500–1100* (Oxford: Oxford University Press, 2017), 217: "While it [the Church] never opposed slavery fundamentally, it *was* concerned that it should not be incompatible with salvation or living a Christian life."

33. See also Danaë Simmermacher, *Eigentum als ein subjektives Recht bei Luis de Molina (1535–1600). Dominium und Sklaverei in De Iustitia et Iure* (Berlin and Boston: de Gruyter, 2018), 206–18.

34. Molina, *DIEI*, II.38.5: "Inter dominum et servum, non qua servus est, sed qua homo, cui accidit, ut sit servus, esse potest contractus."

35. Aristotle, *Politics* I, 5, 1254a16–1255a1.

war.[36] Based largely on the legal tradition of Roman Law, Molina discusses a number of reasons that he believes would lead to a form of legal enslavement that he calls *just titles*.

The first title, and the most important for Molina's general argument, is based on the norms applicable in a just war: "The first title is the right of war (*ius belli*), such as when someone is captured in a just war. By the law of nations, one becomes a slave of those who captured him, commuting his death for perpetual slavery" (disputation 33, 1). Although this rule applies primarily to combatants on the unjust side in a war, in some cases it is admissible to enslave noncombatants (*innocentes*).[37]

The second argument states that a person can be reduced to slavery as punishment for a crime he has committed. Supplying enemies with arms, rebellion, or being ungrateful after having been released by an owner would make the person deserving of such punishment (disputation 33, 4). This argument also applies to enslavement by birth (disputation 33, 32). Although this might seem to be a version of natural slavery, Molina rather sees it as an extension of the previous argument, giving it a decidedly political tone. Although children are innocent at birth, they are the object of the father's punishment. Moreover, once the children grow up, they may actively participate in hostilities and therefore it is licit to preempt that possibility. The case that Molina discusses in this context is the Morisco uprising in Granada from 1569 to 1571. In his view, the Morisco population constituted a kind of republic against which it would be legitimate to wage war and to punish the crimes committed or likely to be committed.

The third title is purchase and sale (disputation 33, 14), which takes two forms: self-sale and the sale of someone already enslaved. Self-sale rests on the assumption that the person selling himself "is not only the owner of his honor and reputation but also has ownership of his own freedom so that even by natural right alone, he could alienate this freedom and reduce himself to slavery" (disputation 33, 14). Human beings can exercise free agency not only over external goods, such as furniture,

---

36. Aristotle, *Politics* I, 6, 1255a6–10.

37. Theological consensus at the time exempted enemy Christian war prisoners from enslavement by Christian captors. Molina concurs in DIEI II.117.4. It was a point of debate whether this privilege extended also to Christian heretics.

but also over goods that, in a significant way, constitute what the person is: honor, reputation, and freedom. Molina seems to think that in some circumstances it might be reasonable to voluntarily relinquish a part of one's freedom. For Molina, six conditions must be met for self-sale and subjection to voluntary slavery to be considered valid: "First, that the person being sold is over twenty years of age. Second, that he knows he is free at the time he is sold. Third, that he allows himself to be sold by another so that he may receive a part of the price paid.[38] Fourth, that he actually receives part of the price paid. Fifth, that the person who sells him knows that he is free. Sixth, that the person who buys him knows that he is a slave" (disputation 33, 16).

An extension of this argument is when parents sell their own children in cases of extreme, life-threatening hardship (disputation 33, 27–28). As cruel as this view sounds, Molina does not believe that slavery is permanent in these circumstances, because the conditions may improve and the paterfamilias may be able to pay a fee to recover the child. In fact, the sale of the child is in the child's best interest, because in the circumstances in which such a sale is allowed, the parents are unable to feed the child, and, as a slave, the chances of survival increase considerably. As with the previous just titles for enslavement, Molina not only appeals to the body of legal texts he copiously cites but also to the historical, social, and geographical evidence he has gathered on the subject of poverty and almsgiving in Europe and in places as far away as India. He also considers cases in which enslavement serves to protect the innocent from an injustice, such as anthropophagy. In such cases, the person in question might be bought but the option of regaining freedom by paying a price is left open.

The fourth title is that of the condition of birth (disputation 33, 32). Referring again to Roman Law, Molina states that "whoever is born from an enslaved mother is a slave, whether his father is free or not, whether he is born from a legitimate marriage or from fornication"

---

38. "To participate in the price" may be understood as "participating in setting the price"; however, we think it makes more sense to read it as translated above. See also William Warwick Buckland, *The Roman Law of Slavery: The Condition of the Slave in Private Law from Augustus to Justinian* (Cambridge: Cambridge University Press, 1908), 432.

(disputation 33, 32). The idea that "birth follows the womb" (*partus sequitur ventrem*) holds the assumption that the status of the mother applies to an unborn child as well. In appearance this is a variation of natural slavery, because such children have no other option than to be permanently enslaved, since they are locked into slavery without the option of buying back their own freedom, as in the title of self-sale or the sale of children in case of grave necessity.[39]

Molina's Analysis of the Slave Trade

The main focus of Molina's treatise is the incipient slave trade from Upper Guinea and Central West Africa to Brazil. As a Jesuit priest, he was not only interested in determining the facts based on accounts he received but also in establishing whether the merchants and ultimately the buyers of slaves could proceed in "safe conscience." However, the concern about maintaining a safe conscience with its implications for the prospects of salvation also applied to political authorities. For example, could the Portuguese king and the royal court have a safe conscience knowing that the slave trade was being conducted in a morally deficient way?

Apart from the monarch, Molina divides the participants in the slave trade into three main groups: (1) the intermediaries on African soil, called *tangosmãos* or *pombeiros*; (2) the merchants who sell slaves in ports such as Cape Verde; and (3) the customers who acquire the slaves on the European or American mainland. Most of disputations 34 through 36 are devoted to the various theoretical and practical challenges posed by a series of epistemic and moral considerations.

Molina goes on to examine the Portuguese merchants' claim that they acquired slaves by purchase according to a legal practice. He argues that, "for the Portuguese to own them by a title of sale or barter, it is necessary that they [initially] be reduced to slavery by some other title unless one of them happens to be bought by the Portuguese to

39. For an additional thorough analysis of the four reasons for enslavement, see Matthias Kaufmann, "Slavery between Law, Morality, and Economy," in *A Companion to Luis de Molina*, ed. Mathias Kaufmann and Alexander Aichele, 183–225, specifically 194ff.

save him from a just or unjust death" (disputation 34, 3). This means that the legality of any transfer of property depends on the legality of the original acquisition. If a slave was first acquired illegally, this would taint any subsequent transaction with illegality.

The legality of the Portuguese acquisition of slaves on the African mainland rested on the assumption that the slaves were soldiers fighting a war for the unjust side against a just side. Only if this were the case could any further trade be legal.

The *tangosmãos* were Portuguese merchants who operated on the mainland in Upper Guinea, which encompassed the coasts of present-day Senegal to Liberia, while *pombeiros* did the same in Central West Africa, in what is now the coastal region of Congo and Angola. After establishing themselves in the vicinity of local chieftains or *sobas*, they were able to buy slaves directly "at the source." It is evident that Molina did not think highly of these merchants because they did not attempt to determine whether the people they acquired had been justly reduced to slavery by the *sobas* from whom they bought them:

The Portuguese merchants (whether those who dock their ships in different places to do business or those called *pombeiros* who go into the inner regions in search of goods or other inhabitants of the realms of Angola or Mani-congo) do not care about the titles [under which these persons have been enslaved] nor do they ask how they were enslaved, when they were sold, or whether they have already been reduced [to slavery]; they take all the slaves without distinction as long as a price is agreed upon. (disputation 34, 14)

According to Molina, the evidence suggests that the *sobas* would usually raid villages and kidnap some of the inhabitants to be sold to the Portuguese. This obviously calls into question the morality of the slave trade from the very beginning: If the initial act of appropriation is already questionable, then the subsequent deals are questionable as well. If this was indeed the case, then, Molina argues, the merchants should restore the slaves' freedom and pay for the damage they caused. This line of argument also applies when another form of slave acquisition—a parent selling his child in extreme necessity—is surrounded by doubts. If it turns out that the necessity was not extreme, then the enslavement and any subsequent transferences would be illegitimate.

The merchants who bought slaves from the *tangosmãos* or *pombeiros* should therefore exercise what Molina calls due moral diligence (*diligentia moralis* or *debita*); that is, they should strive to obtain as much certainty as possible about the origin of the slaves they bought. Molina's view resembles contemporary views on the ethics of international trade and consumer choice, such as the immorality of selling and purchasing blood diamonds, while diamonds from morally "safe" sources can be traded legally. Analogously, Molina was interested in pointing out what a legal and ethical slave trade would look like—one that could be conducted by merchants with a safe conscience.

Also in disputation 34, Molina takes a close look at other regions on the African continent, and relies on reports from India, China, and Japan on the different ways in which slaves were incorporated into social life and commerce. His main concern is the slave trade, which he generally treats as morally suspect. However, due to local political and social customs and beliefs, in Molina's view, the purchase of slaves by foreigners can sometimes be legitimate. For example, when reflecting on the Japanese wars, Molina suggests that, if these wars were based on a complete mutual disregard for the justice of the reasons for going to war, then the captured soldiers could become legitimate objects of trade.

The lack of scruples among slave merchants did not detract from Molina's optimistic attitude toward normal business practices. He believed that people could usually trust each other, that commercial transactions could generally be assumed to be legitimate, and that people tended to operate on the basis of good faith (*bona fides*). Good faith is a core element of Molina's business ethics. Under Roman Law, a person who holds something in good faith for a sufficient period of time can be treated as the owner for legal purposes, even if ownership cannot be proven by documents.[40]

In cases where absolute certitude about the titles of ownership is lacking, good faith allows the parties to engage in a lawful exchange. In the case of the slave trade, secondary purchasers of slaves who bought them in good faith from a merchant, believing in the legality of the original enslavement, were not liable for damages to the slaves if it turned out that their original enslavement was in fact unjust. However,

40. D. L. Carey Miller, "Property," in *A Companion to Justinian's Institutes*, ed. Ernest Metzger (London: Duckworth, 1997), 48.

if they doubted the legality of the original enslavement and thus did not buy the slave in good faith, the slave had a claim against them for the loss of his freedom and the fruits of his labor that were unjustly taken.

The main thrust of Molina's arguments was to establish whether a merchant who originally bought or resold a slave could enjoy the rights afforded by acting in good faith. His view was that

[b]y buying them without inquiring into the title under which they were subjected to slavery and without a just cause for rejecting the presumption that suggests or could suggest the contrary, he effectively sins mortally. He would not possess them in good faith, but he would be bound to inquire about the truth as often as the opportunity arises. (disputation 35, 16)

All of this leaves the merchants in a moral predicament. The only way to avoid guilt and to be able to receive absolution from a confessor would be to have met the following conditions: (1) the person reduced to slavery was justly reduced, for example by the right of war, especially by what is called *ius in bello*; (2) the war was just on the side that captured the soldier; and (3) the merchant must exercise due moral diligence to establish these facts (ignorance of morally relevant data does not excuse a person unless that ignorance is "invincible," the kind of ignorance that could not possibly have been avoided). Molina suggests that sometimes the right course of action is neither a full restitution of the slave's freedom nor continued enslavement but something in between. Depending on the degree of doubt (*pro quantitate dubii*) as to the legality of the original acquisition of the slave's freedom, the slaveholder might be obliged to restore a part of that freedom or a certain amount of money.

Molina's analysis of the rights of slave merchants takes stock of the moral ambiguities of the trade but does not align with modern moral sensibilities, which abhor slavery as such. Rights can be attributed to merchants in Molina's view because slavery is based on a legitimate model of ownership (*dominium proprietatis*), but this requires meeting various epistemic requirements concerning the acquisition and selling of slaves, such as knowing and acknowledging that the slave was legally bought and no local laws or customs have been violated. These were difficult conditions to meet.

When Molina addressed the Portuguese slave trade, he joined an ongoing controversy. Discussions of slavery and the slave trade were often a part of treatments on commutative justice or the justice of exchanges, under the heading of ownership.

Earlier well-known discussions on the Portuguese slave trade can be found in Tomás de Mercado (1525–75) and Bartolomé Frías de Albornoz (1519–73).[41] Discussions can also be found in other earlier authors such as Francisco de Vitoria,[42] Domingo de Soto,[43] Pedro Navarra,[44] Martín de Ledesma[45] and, more extensively, in Miguel de Palacio,[46] Luis López,[47] and Francisco García.[48] Moral denunciations of the slave trade were not limited to theologians. In a letter to the king of Portugal, a bishop of Santiago in Cape Verde openly denounced that, "out of a thousand slaves in this kingdom, nine hundred have been unjustly captured."[49] Molina's exhaustive, fact-informed analysis of the

41. Tomás de Mercado, *Summa de tratos y contratos* (Sevilla: Fernando Díaz, 1587), lib. 2, cap. 20, fols. 102–17, and Bartolomé de Albornóz, *Arte de los contratos* (Valencia: Pedro de Huarte, 1573) tit. 4, fols. 130b–131a.

42. Francisco de Vitoria, "Letter to Bernardino Vique," in *Vitoria: Political Writings*, ed. Anthony Pagden and Jeremy Lawrance (Cambridge: Cambridge University Press, 1991). Vique was the Dominical Provincial. He was later murdered along with a slave by assassins hired by a local count.

43. Domingo de Soto, *De la justicia y el derecho*, Spanish trans. by P. Marcelino Gonzáles Ordóñez (Madrid: Instituto de Estudios Políticos, 1967), with fascimile of *De iustitia et iure*, Salamanca 1556 edition, lib. 4, q. 2, a. 2, at 289.

44. Pedro de Navarra, *De ablatorum restitutione in foro conscientiae* (Toledo: Tomás Guzmán, 1597), lib. 3, chap. 1, n. 196 at 151–58.

45. Martin de Ledesma, *Secunda quartae* (Coimbra: Juan Álvarez, 1560), q. 18, a. 1, dub. 11., fol. 225.

46. Miguel de Palacio, *Praxis theologica de contractibus et restitutionibus* (Salamanca: Juan Fernández, 1585), lib. 2, c. 10 at 151–57.

47. Luis López, *De contractibus et negotiationibus* (Venice: Apud Iuntas, 1593 c. 1589), lib. 1, c. 5 at 20–22.

48. Francisco García, *Tratado utilísimo y muy general de todos los contratos* (Valencia: Ioan Navarro, 1583), chap. 17 at 490–92.

49. "Carta do Bispo de Cabo Verde a el Rey," in *África Ocidental (1570–1600)*, vol. 3 of *Monumenta Missionaria Africana. Segunda Série*, ed. Antonio Brásio (Lisbon: Agencia-Geral do Ultramar, 1964), 442. The bishop in question may have been the Carmelite Pedro Brandão, who, according to some, was himself dismissed and sent back to Portugal for trading in slaves.

slave trade soon became indispensable for later authors such as Fernando Rebello,[50] Antonino Diana,[51] Tomás Sánchez,[52] Juan de Salas,[53] Egidio Trullench,[54] Sebastião Fagundez,[55] Tomás Hurtado,[56] and Luis de Caspe.[57]

Molina's critical stance on the Portuguese slave trade, however, was not universally accepted. While Portuguese theologians were the first to take issue with Molina, they were soon joined by Spanish authors. Spain's increasing involvement in the slave trade and the dynastic union between Portugal and Spain from 1580 to 1640 contributed to this. Initially, authors who supported the slave trade were not critical of Molina. For instance, the Portuguese Jesuit Fernando Rebello, who had earlier helped Molina improve his Latin, rather than oppose his general account, attempted in a work published in 1608 to use several of his arguments to help justify the Portuguese trade while ignoring Molina's more overt criticisms.[58] Rebello applied Molina's criteria for just slavery in a much more liberal way, lowering the requirements needed for a slave owner to qualify as a good faith possessor of the slave.

However, there were limits to the extent to which Molina's text could be used against its original intent. The main moral obstacle concerned the slaves brought from the Cap-Vert (the peninsula where

50. Fernando Rebello, *Opus de obligationibus* (Lyon: Cardon, 1608), lib. 1, q. 10, sec. 1 at 69–74.

51. Antonino Diana, *Coordinatus, seu Omnes resolutiones morales* (Lyon: Jean-Antoine Huguetan, 1680), pt. 7, tract. 8, resol. 8 at 431–32.

52. Tomás Sánchez, *Consilia seu opuscula moralia* (Lyon: Prost, 1643), vol. 1, book 1, chap. 1, dub. 4 at 4.

53. Juan de Salas, "De contractu lusitanorum ementium aethiopes" in Juan de la Peña. *De bello contra insulanos*, vol. 2, 14–18, *Corpus Hispanorum de Pace*, vol. 9 (Madrid: C.S.I.C., 1982), 408.

54. Egidio Trullench, *Operis moralis, tomus secundus* (Lyon: Anisson, 1652), book 7, dub. 8 at 124.

55. Sebastião Fagundez, *De iustitia et contractibus* (Lyon: Annison and Boissat, 1641), book 2, chaps. 1–4 at 145–53.

56. Tomás Hurtado, *Tractatus varii resolutionum moralium, pars posterior* (Lyon: Annison, 1651), tract. 8, chap. 3, digression 1, q. 10 at 81–88 (second pagination).

57. Luis de Caspe, *Cursus theologicus* (Lyon: Boissat and Anisson, 1643), tract. 18, d. 5, a. 2 at 206.

58. On Rebello's help to Molina see Molina to Acquaviva, October 30, 1583, in Stegmüller, *Molinismus*, 570, line 25.

Dakar is today, not to be confused with the Cape Verde islands) and Lower and Upper Guinea. There, unlike what happened in the territories that the Portuguese referred to as the kingdoms of Angola, Manicongo, and Monomotapa (roughly in today's Angola, the coast of the Republic of the Congo, and northern Zimbabwe, respectively), there was no war between Portugal and any African polity such that it could provide a moral justification for the enslavement of war captives. And it was precisely from these regions that most slaves came. The argument that slaves were simply innocent human beings who have been hunted down as beasts seemed incontrovertibly true with respect to these areas.

The Portuguese Jesuit Sebastião Fagundez, writing in 1641 in response to the condemnation of "our merchants" by writers "from other nations," set out to question the information provided by Molina about Cap-Vert and the Guineas and tried to unearth facts to justify the enslavement of people from those areas. It is clear that, for Fagundez, Molina's description of the political, social, and juridical realities was unhelpful to Portuguese commercial interests and was seen as the source of the moral opprobrium suffered by its merchants. Fagundez echoes the arguments presented by Giovanni Pietro Maffei's chronicle of Portuguese exploration, *Historiarum Indicarum* (1588), in which the inhabitants of Cap-Vert and the Guineas are described as having been born "for servitude." He also argues that slaves would only improve their situation by moving "from the deserts of Ethiopia" (a generic term for sub-Saharan Africa) to opulent Lisbon, a city where all human needs are abundantly met.[59]

A Spanish opponent of Molina, Tomás Hurtado, argued that slave buyers were morally exempt from inquiring into the justice of the enslavement of the people they purchased. He did this by drawing a parallel between the slave buyer and the situation of a soldier called to war, who, according to Molina himself, does not have to make an independent inquiry into the justice of the war.[60] The parallel is

---

59. Giovanni Pietro Maffei, *Historiarum indicarum libri XVI* (Vienna: Trattneriana, 1752), 6.

60. Tomás Hurtado, *Tractatus varii resolutionum moralium, pars posterior* (Lyon: Anisson, 1651), tract. 8, chap. 3, sec. 2, n. 306 at 83–84 (second pagination).

obviously misleading. Slave buyers did not buy slaves out of obedience to a superior, nor did they face any moral risk by failing to buy slaves, unlike soldiers who face the moral risk of not defending their country in a just war if they fail to fight.

Synopsis of the Translated Disputations

In disputation 32, Molina addresses the fundamental moral and legal underpinnings of slavery beginning with conceptual issues. What kind of servitude is slavery? Can slavery be lawful? Is it allowed by the Scriptures? Is it contrary to natural law?

In disputation 33, Molina goes on to consider what he calls the "titles" of just slavery, namely the ways in which a person can be justly enslaved, drawing primarily on Roman Law. For Molina, there are four basic types of justly enslaved people: combatants captured in a just war (*mancipia*), adults who voluntarily sell their freedom, those who have had a severe just punishment commuted by slavery or have had slavery as a punishment, and those whose mothers were slaves. Molina also considers adventitious ways of becoming a slave, such as when children are sold by their parents or as a means for a freed person to repay his captor. Along the way, Molina discusses actual cases of his time, such as the enslavement of the Morisco children after the rebellion of the Morisco population in southern Spain in 1568–71.[61]

The next disputation, 34, is the longest in Molina's discussion. It intertwines several elements: an account of the beginning and development of the Portuguese trade in African slaves beginning in 1446; a description of the various African geopolitical units as perceived by the Portuguese; a detailed description of the mechanics of the slave trade, including an account of the role of African and Portuguese intermediaries; and the taxation regime of the slave trade and the use of barter to purchase slaves. Crucially, Molina includes scathing criticism of the absolute indifference about the origins of slaves, not only among Portuguese traders but also among Portuguese ecclesiastical and local

---

61. On late Scholastic views on the slavery of Morisco children, see Daniel Schwartz, *The Political Morality of the Late Scholastics: Civic Life, War and Conscience* (Cambridge: Cambridge University Press, 2019), 197–206.

political authorities especially on the island of São Tomé (then the main slave trading post as well as a site of slave-based agriculture).

These elements emerge as Molina systematically tells the reader about the political, social, and legal characteristics, to the best of his knowledge, of different African populations. He begins with the Muslim Wolof people of present-day Senegal, then moves on to the inhabitants of the two Guineas; the kingdoms (or, as he describes them, the loose groupings of small kingdoms) of Angola, Manicongo, and Sofala (now in Mozambique) and the region called Cafreria. Cafreria was the coastal area on the southern tip of Africa, from which the derogatory Spanish term *cafre* was derived. Originally describing someone uneducated and rude, it was derived from the Arabic word *kaffir*, meaning a denier of the Islamic faith. Finally, he mentions Monomotapa. For each of these areas Molina examines whether there are any circumstances in place that allow for just enslavement, which he finds only in those places where the Portuguese could be thought to be waging a just war against local rulers, such as in Angola, the Congo River basin, and Sofala. According to Molina, slaves from other African regions should be presumed to have been unjustly reduced to slavery.

Molina offers an analysis of the social stratification of some African societies, including the local use of slaves, their—in his view—corrupt administration of justice, their intracommunal and intercommunal strife, and the ways in which the failings of local rulership and the suffering of their subjects had been greatly exacerbated by the profits that African rulers could now reap from Portugal's insatiable demand for slaves.

Molina did not stop with Africa. The Portuguese also traded in slaves from Asia. He goes on to discuss the Kingdom of Calicut (Kozhikode, on the Malabar coast), Sumatra, Malacca, Java, Ceylon (Sri Lanka), Cambodia, Pegu (the Hanthawaddy kingdom in present-day Myanmar), China, and Japan. He devotes most of his attention to India, China, and Japan. Each of these places presented different political and social circumstances relevant to possible justifications for slavery. Most interesting is Molina's analysis of Japan during the Sengoku, or Warring States, period (1467–1568), when warlords fought each other without, according to Molina, even pretending to have a just cause.

Disputation 35 is less factual. It contains Molina's moral assessment of the Portuguese slave trade. Molina begins by explaining his motives: to get advisors close to the Portuguese king, such as his confessors, to persuade him to have the issue of the slave trade examined by learned men. This was particularly important because there was a long-standing tradition of writers who condemned the trade as constituting a mortal sin. In other words, his goal was to get the king to appoint a commission similar to the one in Valladolid summoned by the Spanish king in 1550 that examined the justice of the conquest of the Americas so that a pronouncement could be made on the matter of the slave trade.

Molina devotes the first two sections of the disputation to the prohibition by the Spanish monarchs of the enslavement of Indigenous peoples of the Americas and the exemption from slavery of the Morisco children. Regarding the first part, it is true that Charles V issued a series of decrees against the unjust enslavement of the Indigenous American population, the most important of which were the New Laws of 1542.[62] However, the *encomienda* was a system of forced labor that in many ways resembled slavery. It survived well into the seventeenth century (vestigial forms persisted into the eighteenth century) and was not officially abolished until the colonies became politically independent. Moreover, both directly and through intermediaries (through what was called the *asiento* system), Spain was heavily involved during Molina's time in the African slave trade.[63] Some estimates say that 68,500 Africans had been trafficked by Spanish vessels to Spanish America by 1581.[64] Molina's reference to the Spanish monarchs reveals that, beneath the surface of the controversy over slavery, national antagonisms between Spain and Portugal were still playing a role.

The main justification for enslavement was based on the just war theory. Molina acknowledged that more often than not, doubts may

62. On the Spanish crown's attempts to put an end to slavery in Spanish America, see Jesús María García Añoveros, "Carlos V y la abolición de la esclavitud de los indios: Causas, evolución y circunstancias," *Revista de Indias* 60 (2000): 58–84.

63. On Spanish involvement in the trade of African slaves, see Alex Borucki, David Eltis, and David Wheat, "Atlantic History and the Slave Trade to Spanish America," *American Historical Review* 120 (2015): 440.

64. See David Eltis and David Richardson, eds., *Atlas of the Transatlantic Slave Trade* (New Haven: Yale University Press, 2010), 23.

arise as to the question of whether a just war actually took place and whether a merchant who has bought a slave in good faith is guilty if it cannot be determined whether the slave was captured in a just war. Disputation 36 thus deals with the moral uncertainty of purchasing and selling slaves after their enslavement. It focuses on the application to slavery of the legal principle that privileges the claims of a de facto possessor in cases of doubtful ownership. The principle applies as long as the possession is acquired in good faith. It follows that a merchant cannot possess a slave in good faith and thus enjoy the privilege of being a good faith possessor unless he examines whether the slave has been justly enslaved. If not, then the merchant must restore the slave's freedom independently of the price paid.

Disputation 37 raises another issue: Assuming the legitimacy of enslavement, such as that conducted in a just war, would it be permissible for a slave to escape from bondage? The general answer is no. Consider the act of selling oneself, for which Molina sets strict conditions: it would be a breach of contract if someone unilaterally decided to cancel it.[65] In general, the legitimacy of legal or moral norms, such as those that are derived from the *ius gentium*, is not to be questioned, and therefore any action contrary to these norms must be considered wrong. Thus, escape from just enslavement is wrong and the slave could be forced to return to his owner.

The rights of owners with respect to a slave are the subject of disputation 38. This text is particularly thought-provoking. In the first place, and in accordance with the principle that human beings are only guardians and not owners in the strict sense of life and limb, it is considered wrong to kill or to maim a slave. Molina goes on to set a series of minimal criteria for a humane life for the slave, that is, that he be seen "not inasmuch as he is a slave but because he is a human being who happens to be a slave" (disputation 38, 5). It follows that a slave should be allowed to pursue private interests, such as signing contracts and marrying.

Disputation 39 discusses several ways to free a slave. First, a slave may redeem himself for a fixed price. Second, if a slave is denied food,

---

65. See Danaë Simmermacher, *Eigentum als ein subjektives Recht bei Luis de Molina*, 203, and Costello, *The Political Philosophy of Luis de Molina*, 168–69.

it may be permissible for others to set him free to preserve his life. Third, slaves could be freed if it was reported to the bishop that they had been sexually exploited. Molina discusses six additional ways of regaining legal freedom.

Disputation 40 deals with a different modality of slave liberation. It concerns the question of whether a Christian slave of an apostate or heretic must be freed when the owner has been condemned by the Inquisition. The basic question is fiscal in nature and asks whether Christian slaves, previously considered property, become the property of the Crown or whether they should obtain their freedom. Based on an instruction promulgated in 1484 by Ferdinand and Isabella, and in accordance with the general idea that Christians should never be slaves of non-Christians, Molina argues that heretics automatically lose their ownership of slaves when condemned by the Inquisition.

Brief Remarks on This Translation

For this translation, we were fortunate to be able to rely on an edition of the text as edited by Matthias Kaufmann, Danaë Simmermacher, and Alexander Loose. We were also able to compare our own translation with the German contained in that edition and with the Spanish translation by Fraga Iribarne. Although both were helpful, we must emphasize that our translation is based directly on the Latin text. We have tried to provide a conceptually accurate version, while at the same time providing a text that can be read without reproducing the some-times-convoluted Latin syntax for which Molina is sometimes feared. Not being an *ad litteram* translation, we have sometimes chosen to break up long sentences into smaller units, thus hopefully allowing for a clearer understanding of the meaning of Molina's discussions.

Some of the choices we have made in our translation need to be briefly explained. First, the technical term *dominium proprietatis* is consistently translated as "ownership." Contrary to the common translation of *dominus* as "master" or "lord," we wanted to convey its legal meaning related to the contractual aspects of ownership, so we used the noun "owner." The Latin word *filius*, which means "son," we have mostly translated as "child" or "children," because in most contexts

Molina seems to think of boys and girls alike. When referring to sub-Saharan Africans, Molina follows the usage of his time, and uses the word Aethiopes. We translate this as "Africans." *Servus* and *mancipium*, although having different connotations stemming from ancient legal traditions, are both translated as "slave." Molina frequently speaks of *doctores*, which we translate as "jurists." And to maintain consistency, the noun *libertas* is uniformly translated as "freedom," also because the adjective *liber* is translated as "free." The numbers between parentheses in the text are as they are in the original text, but we have omitted the notes in the margins.

Disputation 32

On slaves and, first of all, whether one human being
can acquire ownership of another

Summary

1. What is natural slavery?
2. On legal slavery.
3. Why slaves are called captured slaves (*mancipia*).
4. The slavery of domestic servants.
5. The lawful slavery of captured slaves.
6. That a slave must not spurn his master in matters of religion.
7. Whether slavery is contrary to natural law.

Now that we have explained jurisdiction (*dominio jursidictionis*),
we must now discuss ownership (*dominium proprietatis*). But, because
the nature of this matter is made up of interrelated parts, much has
already been said while we were discussing ownership in general, and
now we must explain the various legitimate causes [*tituli*] and ways
that it [ownership] is acquired and lost. I will speak as much about
ownership itself as about the right of property and Civil Law. First of
all, we must examine whether one person is able to have not only jurisdictional ownership but also ownership of another and with what titles
the ownership of this kind is acquired and lost.

(1) This ownership is a certain relationship with a slave, not just any
slave, but a civil and legal slave, as Aristotle calls it. To understand this
matter, one must know that slavery is twofold, as Aristotle teaches in

chapters 3 and 4 of book I of the *Politics*.[1] There is a certain suitability, which is called natural, by which duller and rougher people tend to be physically stronger. There are some who are more suited by their own nature to obey and, as a result, they are governed by others for their own good, just as there are those more suited for command and governance. However, this suitability is incorrectly called slavery, [and it is so called] not because it grants some other person a right over this kind of people but rather because of a certain equity, since the nature of the thing itself demands that [these people] subject themselves of their own accord to wiser and finer people. This is only so that they may be ruled and governed for their own good by those men. These [slaves], in turn, repay them with obedience, reverence, and honor or even allegiance and other kinds of support, and accordingly they have subjected themselves to a regime either kingly or of some other sort. (2) Another kind of slavery is that which Aristotle calls civil and legal because slaves in this category are bound to their owners (*domines*) for the works and benefits that can be obtained from them. This kind of people, as *Institutiones De iure personarum*, section *Servi*, says, are called slaves by virtue of their service, (3) because those whom the emperors have captured in war and whom it was legal to kill, were enslaved, their death having been commuted to perpetual slavery.[2] As this text adds, these [people] are also called captured *mancipia* as if they had been physically taken from the hands (*ab manu capta*) of their enemies.[3] So, it would seem that this slavery has also been introduced for the good of the slaves themselves, inasmuch as perpetual slavery is a lesser evil for them than being deprived of life. (4) Domestic slavery is a kind of middle ground between these two kinds of slavery since these slaves are hired for a wage to perform specific tasks and to give allegiance, which does not establish ownership but only [generates] the right to their work and their type of service. In the matter to be discussed, we will therefore only discuss the second type of slavery, in which slaves are called slaves in relation to the owners who exert ownership over them.

1. Actually, Aristotle refers to slavery in *Politics* I, 2–3.

2. Justinian, *Institutiones*, ed. Paul Krueger (Berlin: Wiedmann, 1867), 1.3.

3. Here Molina stresses the etymological relation between *servus* and *ab manu capta*. In the current translation *servus* and *mancipium* will be generally translated as *slave*.

(5) It is clear enough that this type of slavery is lawful and just as long as there are legitimate titles. This is not only the common opinion of scholars on the basis of both Civil and Canon Law (*Liber extra, De coniugio servorum*, throughout the book),[4] and of that first origin from which slavery is said to have been introduced, but also based on the sacred scriptures. In Leviticus 25, God commanded the people of Israel thus: "If thy brother, constrained by poverty, sell himself to thee: thou shalt not oppress him with the service of bondservants. But he shall be as a hireling, and a sojourner he shall work with thee until the year of the jubilee. And afterward he shall go out with his children: and shall return to his kindred and to the possession of his fathers. For they are my servants, and I brought them out of the land of Egypt: let them not be sold as bondmen."[5] Yet he would subjugate others as slaves: "Let your bondmen, and your bondwomen, be of the nations that are round about you: And of the strangers that sojourn among you, or that were born of them in your land. These you shall have for servants: And by right of inheritance shall leave them to your posterity and shall possess them forever."[6] In 1 Timothy, 6, [Paul says]: "Whosoever are servants under the yoke, let them count their masters worthy of all honor. But they that have believing masters, let them not despise them, because they are brethren; but serve them rather, because they are faithful. These things teach and exhort. If any man teach otherwise and consent not to the sound words, he is proud, knowing nothing."[7] In 1 Corinthians, 7 [he says]: "Let every man abide in the same calling in which he was called. Wast thou called, being a bondman? Care not for it: but if thou mayest be made free, use it rather."[8] The same thing is seen in Ephesians 5, Colossians 3 and 4, Philemon, and 1 Peter 2.

---

4. *Liber extra,* in *Corpus iuris canonici*, vol. 2, ed. Emil Friedberg and Aemilius Ludwig Richter (Leipzig: Bernhard Tauchnitz, 1881), X.4.9.

5. *The Holy Bible, Douay-Rheims Version, Translated from the Latin Vulgate* (2009). Lv 25:39–42. In this book, we use a modern English translation of the Latin version of the Old Testament that Molina read and was the official version for Catholics at the time, the Vulgate. Most modern English translations are not from the Latin Vulgate but rather from the Septuagint.

6. Lv 25:44–46.

7. 1 Tm 6:1–4. The quotation is incomplete.

8. 1 Cor 7:20–21.

(6) The same [i.e., that slavery can be just and licit] was decided in the Council of Gangra in these words [chapter *Si quis servum*, 17, q. 4]: "If anyone teaches a foreign slave to condemn his master and to forsake his post for reasons of religion, and he could not have better taught him to serve his master in good faith and with all honor, let him be anathema."[9] The same definition on this matter is contained in the chapter *Si quis servum*, 2, from the council of Pope Martin.

(7) But what if someone objects on the basis of the law *Libertas, ff. De statu hominum, & ss. servitus, Instituta De iure personarum* [and states] that in these texts it is said that slavery comes from the law of nations from which it follows that a person being owned by someone is contrary to nature?[10] From this one might gather that slavery is illicit inasmuch as it is against the law of nature. I should say that these words mean that slavery, if one were to consider the original state of things alone, without considering the circumstances by which slavery was justified, is against nature, since remaining in the sole original state of things, we would all be free by nature itself. But, with intervening circumstances, slavery is justified, and it was lawfully and justly introduced by the law of nations against what the first state of things alone established. Read what I have discussed in disputation 20 about the division of things (*divisio rerum*) as well as in treatise 1, disputation 4.[11]

9. In Cuthbert Hamilton Turner, *Ecclesiae occidentalis monumenta iuris antiquissima: Concilia Gangrense et Antiochenum* (Oxford: Clarendon, 1907), vol. 2, pt. 2, can. LXI at 186.

10. Dig., book 1, title 5, paragraph 4. *Corpus Iuris Civilis*, ed. Mommsen and Krueger.

11. Here we follow the way *divisio rerum* is translated in the *Corpus Iuris Civilis*. Often it is referred to as private property.

Disputation 33

The titles by which ownership over slaves may justly be obtained and whether the children of those who rebelled in the Kingdom of Granada could justly be reduced to slavery

Summary

1. The first title of slavery: The right of war.

2. A Christian does not become a slave to a Christian by the right of war, even though he does to an infidel.

3. In just war, innocent children and others become slaves even if they cannot be killed lawfully.

4. The second title of slavery: When someone is condemned to slavery because of an offense.

5. How those fall into slavery who have married having been earlier initiated in some sacred order and even the children that came from such a marriage, also on those who give arms and other assistance to the Saracens and also on ungrateful freedmen, as well as on abductors and the abducted.

6. Rebels and apostates in the Kingdom of Granada are to be conscripted into slavery but their underage children are exempt.

7. Whether the king in conscience had to exempt the aforementioned underage children; the affirmative argument is first established.

8. The second argument.

9. The author establishes the first negative argument.

10. The second.

11. The third.

12. Response to the first argument of the affirmative opinion.

13. To the second.

14. The third title consists in selling oneself into slavery.

15. He who subjects himself to slavery without reasonable cause sins.

16. The six requisite conditions for the valid purchase and sale of a free person.

17. Someone who has become a slave of a buyer cannot redeem himself even for a just price if the buyer is unwilling.

18. If this person is freed for some reason, he does not remain freeborn (*ingenuus*) but rather a freedman (*libertinus*).

19. If any of the aforementioned six conditions are lacking, the purchase is void and a decree of that person's freedom is granted.

20. If someone who is subject to these legal conditions sells himself in a place where these [conditions] are not common or if, inversely, someone who is not subjected to them sells himself where they are common; in either case the sale will be valid.

21. To what extent are parents allowed to sell their children.

22. When those thus sold are freed from slavery, they remain freeborn.

23. A father who comes to greater fortune is required to redeem his child.

24. He cannot sell children who are of age.

25. Nor can he do it when they are married or when they have received sacred orders.

26. Children cannot be sold by their mother.

27. Whether, beyond the case of extreme poverty, when there is an equal or greater cause [than extreme poverty], a father can sell his child.

28. Which are the places where the law regarding the sale of free [children] is valid.

29. When a father or mother sells free [children] by natural right, they cannot redeem them.

30. Someone who is about to be justly killed can lawfully be bought as a slave.

31. To what extent someone who is about to be unjustly killed may be bought.

32. The fourth title of slavery concerns the condition of birth.

This we must establish before anything else: That, after slavery has been legitimately acquired over a slave, the ownership of him is transferred to others by those same titles and means by which ownership of other things is usually transferred, such as by purchase, exchange, grant, last will, etc. Here we will only discuss the titles by which slavery can be legitimately acquired from the beginning and the ownership that can be acquired over a slave.

(1) The first title is the right of war (*ius belli*), such as when someone is captured in a just war. By the law of nations, someone becomes a slave of those who have captured him, commuting his death for perpetual slavery. No one is in doubt about this matter, and there will be a broader discussion below when we discuss war. (2) There is an exception when Christians are captured by other Christians in a just war, as we will discuss in the same place, because this custom is mandatory so that it is a right among Christians that they may not be reduced to slavery. If, however, Christians were to be captured by infidels in a just war waged by the infidels, they would rightly be their slaves because the law of nations applies to all and it would be a commutation of a just death for perpetual slavery, a death that the infidels would be justified in imposing on the Christians who have been captured in this way.

(3) To this title we can add the case of the capture of innocent people, such as infants and others, who are members of the republic against which the just war is being waged. Although they cannot be lawfully killed, by the right of war and the law of nations they may become the slaves of their captors. The reason for this is that, by punishing them, it is as if the republic itself were rightly punished through them as its proper parts regarding all its external goods (*bona fortunae*), one of which is freedom, and this is accepted by common use. However, we will speak of all these things when we come to the subject of war.

(4) The second [title] is the case when someone is condemned to the punishment of slavery by someone who has the power to do so for an offense that, in the judgment of the prudent, is worthy of so great a punishment. For no one is to be punished with slavery for a crime

before a judgment has been passed. What follows will confirm that this title is just. (5) In *Eos qui*, distinction 32, Urban II grants to secular princes the faculty of subjecting to slavery women who have married someone initiated in a sacred order, if they have been admonished by their prelates and yet have not desisted.[1] Likewise, the Ninth Council of Toledo in chapter 15, *Cum multae*, q. 8, decreed that children who were conceived in a reprehensible marriage with those clerics initiated in sacred orders are not only to be completely excluded from the inheritance of their parents but should also be slaves in perpetuity of the church to which the cleric belonged.[2] In the chapter *Ita quorundam de Iudaeis et Saracenis*, Alexander III in the Lateran Council decreed that Christians who supplied Saracens with weapons or timber for the rigs of their galleys or who provided guidance and direction for the piloting of their galleys and pirate ships shall, among other punishments, become the slaves of their captors.[3] Likewise, a freedman who was extremely ungrateful to the person who freed him of his own accord may be returned to slavery as punishment for his offense according to the law *Si manumissus*, chapter *De libertate et eorum liberis, et Instituta De capitis diminutione sectio maxima.*[4] Moreover, in the chapter *De raptoribus*, 36, q. 1, it is established that, if an abductor takes refuge with an abducted woman in a church, and if it is clear that he has taken his victim by force, the abductor may be subjected to slavery, although he retains the right to redeem himself. But if the maiden had previously consented to the abductor and if she had a father, the abductor would be obliged to give her father similar satisfaction.[5]

1. D. 32 c. 10, citing Urban II's canons from the Synod of Melfi, c. 12.

2. See José Vives, ed., *Concilios visigóticos e hispano-romanos* (Barcelona and Madrid: CSIC and Instituto Enrique Flórez, 1963), Ninth Council of Toledo, chap. 10 at 302 (*Quum multae*).

3. *Ita quorundam,* Third Lateran Council (1179), in García y García et al. eds. *Conciliorum oecumenicorum generaliumque decreta* (Turnhout: Brepols, 2013) (CC-COGD, II/I), canon 24 at 144.

4. Cod. 6.7, in *Codex iustinianus,* Krueger ed. (Berlin: Wiedmann, 1877), vol. 1, and Inst.1.16.1–7, in *Corpus Iuris Civilis,* ed. Mommsen and Krueger (Berlin: Wiedmann, 1889).

5. X.5.12.2, in *Corpus Iuris Canonicis,* vol. 2, *Decretalium Collectiones,* ed. Richter and Friedberg (Leipzig: Tauchnitz, 1881), 2nd ed.

(6) In recent years, after those in the Kingdom of Granada who were originally Saracen had rebelled and made themselves apostates of the faith or, rather, openly showed the inner apostasy that they always had in their heart, they were deservedly condemned to the punishment of perpetual slavery for their apostasy and rebellion and the baptism that they had previously received was no impediment [to this].[6] Nevertheless, Philip II, the Catholic king of Spain, enacted a pious law most worthy of his most Christian heart, in which he decreed that the children of the rebels who had not reached the age of puberty at the time of the rebellion or their capture should be granted their freedom as if they were innocent, and this is exactly what he did.

(7) However, it may be doubted whether the king could be bound by conscience to pass such a law. To show the affirmative part of the argument, it may first be argued that these people were innocent. A punishment so great and harsh as slavery cannot be imposed justly unless it were for a crime, especially when the people are baptized, as most of these children were, because nearly all of them had been born before the rebellion.

(8) Second: those who were of Saracen origin in the Kingdom of Granada did not live in a republic separate from the rest of the Spaniards, so that their children would belong to an enemy republic against which a just war could be waged and they could be punished with respect to their external goods, one of which is freedom, as will be seen when the subject of war is analyzed. On the premise that the Saracens in Granada, before their rebellion, did not constitute a republic separate from the rest of the Spaniards but rather one and the same republic under the same ruler, it would undoubtedly have been wrong for the Spaniards to use any right of war against those who did not rebel with

6. Molina is referring to the 1568–71 War of the Alpujarras, an insurrection of the Moriscos, a Spanish population of Muslim descent. In 1572, Felipe II issued a law exempting Morisco children (girls under nine and a half years and boys under ten and a half) from slavery. Most Moriscos were expelled from Spain in 1609. On Morisco slavery, see Aurelia Martín Casares, *La esclavitud en Granada en el siglo XVI* (Granada: Editorial Universidad de Granada, Campus Universitario de Cartuja: Diputación Provincial de Granada, 2000) and William D. Phillips Jr., *Slavery in Medieval and Early Modern Iberia* (Philadelphia: University of Pennsylvania Press, 2014), especially 37–39.

them [that is, the rebellious Saracens], even seizing the temporal goods of these who were completely innocent. On this basis, it can be argued that since the children of the rebels were not part of a republic against which the Spaniards could have waged a just war, and since they, just like their parents, constituted a republic with these same Spaniards, it would have been wrong for the Spaniards to apply any right of war to the children of the rebels by depriving them of their freedom or of other temporal goods, the possession of which belonged to them and not to their parents. Instead, they could only apply the rights of war to those who rebelled.

(9) However, the view that rejects [the Morisco children's right to freedom] seems to be the right one. In fact, the king was not bound by conscience to pass this law; he could have legally condemned all these children to perpetual slavery. I was led [to this view], first of all, because their parents, as soon as they rebelled, elected a king for themselves, and they formed with their children a hostile republic under that ruler against whom the Spaniards could wage a just war as a whole and not only against guilty individuals, which is no different from a war against any other Saracen republic. In fact, that republic, if it had prevailed, would clearly have occupied our lands and taken us captive, children as well as adults. Therefore, just as it is licit for Christians who wage a just war against any other Turkish or Saracen republic to reduce the children they capture to perpetual slavery, thus punishing the republic by depriving it of the good of freedom [i.e., the freedom formerly enjoyed by these children], so the Spaniards were indeed allowed to reduce the children of the hostile republic to slavery. (10) Secondly, although it would be wrong to kill an innocent because of the crime of his parents, it is, however, right to punish him with respect to honor and fame by making him infamous or incapable of many [offices], just as it is licit to punish this innocent with respect to the good of freedom, if the crime of his father were worthy of so great a punishment and if it were expedient for the common good of the republic to strike fear into others.[7] For this reason, according to the chapter *Cum*

---

7. *Infamy* was a legal status that made the infamous ineligible to various civic offices, such as serving in a jury.

multae, 15, q. 8, children who are born of a marriage with someone initiated in sacred orders are subject to slavery for the common good and for the purpose of instilling fear in others.[8] Therefore, since the crimes of apostasy and rebellion committed by rebels in order to remain freely in their infidelity are the gravest sins, these sins should be punished in themselves, as well as to strike fear into others by punishing the perpetrators and also their children for the benefit of the common good. It is consequently [right] that the innocent children of the rebels should be punished with the punishment of perpetual slavery on account of their parents' offense, even if they had not formed with their parents a hostile republic against which the Spaniards could have waged a just war. (11) Thirdly, if it is licit to reduce to slavery the innocent child of a slave by reason of his birth, as the offspring of someone who was justly reduced to slavery because of his own crime or that of his ancestors, why should it not also be just to reduce to slavery his child as his offspring because of the crime of someone who, in order to freely apostatize, rebelled to the greatest detriment of the republic? [This is] all the more so, because in the present case, the father would be punished in the child, and for this reason the punishment would be inflicted on the child for the good of the republic, also in order to strike fear into others. Moreover, the republic could rightly fear that these innocent [children] would follow in the footsteps of their fathers when they came of age because of the children's affection for their parents. For this reason, [the republic] should prudently judge that it is expedient for the common good that those thus enslaved should be distributed among various owners who would take care of them. Nevertheless, while this reasoning alone is not sufficient to subject these innocents to slavery, it does strengthen the preceding arguments.

(12) To the first argument: having conceded the major [premise], it must be said of the minor that, although punishment cannot be justly imposed unless it is because of guilt (*culpa*), the guilt of the republic or of the parents is sometimes sufficient to punish the members of the republic or the children justly with respect to external goods, honor, reputation, or freedom.

---

8. The original has *Cum multu*, 15, q. 8, but the reference seems actually to be to *Cum multae*, chap. 10, of the Ninth Council of Toledo; see note 3 in this chapter.

(13) To the second argument: it has been shown that those who rebelled in the Kingdom of Granada formed with their children a hostile republic under one ruler.[9] Even if they had not formed it, it has been shown that the sins of the parents would have been sufficient to justly reduce their children to slavery. These are the arguments of the second title.

(14) The third title: purchase and sale. In the first place, we must note that a human being, as we have shown in the fourth treatise, is not only the owner of his honor and reputation but also has ownership of his own freedom so that even by natural right alone, he could alienate this freedom and reduce himself to slavery. This is clear not only from the illustrious example of the blessed bishop Paul, who, out of the deepest love for God and his fellow man gave himself in exchange for the freedom of the son of a widow but also from Exodus 21 and Deuteronomy 15 concerning the Hebrew slave who was set free in the seventh year in accordance with the law. Because it was added, "But if he say: I will not depart: because he loveth thee, and thy house, and findeth that he is well with thee: thou shalt take an awl, and bore through his ear in the door of thy house, and he shall serve thee forever."[10] (15) Yet if someone were to squander his freedom, subjecting himself to slavery without a reasonable cause, he would, in fact, sin no less than if he were to squander not only money but also honor and reputation, even without causing scandal.[11] This being thus established, the Imperial Law (excluding the sale by which parents may sell their children, which we shall discuss immediately hereafter) only considers the purchase and sale of a free person as firm and valid according to the six following conditions. (16) First, that the person being sold is over twenty years of age. Second, that he knows he is free at the time he is sold. Third, that he allows himself to be sold by another person so that he may receive a part of the price paid. Fourth, that he actually receives part of the price paid. Fifth, that the person who sells him knows that he

9. The ruler Molina is referring to was Hernando de Valor, later known as Aben Humeya or Ibn Umayya (1520–69).

10. Ex 21:5–6, Dt 15:16–17.

11. Thomas Aquinas in *Summa theologiae*, II-II, q. 43, a. 3, portrays scandal (*scandalum*) as behavior that makes light of admonitions and induces bodily and mostly spiritual devastation on oneself or another person.

is free. Sixth, that the person who buys him knows that he is a slave. (17) When these six conditions occur together, the sale is valid and that person becomes the slave of the one who buys him to the point that, even if the buyer were later offered a fair price for him, he would not be bound to free him. (18) However, if he were to free that person for any reason, he would remain a freedman and not a freeborn person, as he was before. But, if any one of these six conditions is lacking, the sale is void and a proclamation of freedom is granted to the person sold.[12] (19) All this can be established from laws *1 et 4* and *ff., Quibus ad libertatem proclamare non liceat*, the law *Liberis* and *ff., De liberali causa*, the law *Non ideo*, the law *Si ministerium*,[13] codex of the same title *servorum*, and the law *Homo liber* and *ff., De statu hominum*,[14] and from the penultimate section of *Institutiones*,[15] and also from the gloss on *De statu hominum*,[16] together with Antoninus, part 3, title 3, section 5.[17] See also Sylvester and Angelus on the word slavery and the jurists in general.[18] (20) It should be noted that this law is only valid where the Imperial Law is in force. In fact, these laws concern only free men who, being subject to these laws, are allowed to sell themselves to other men who are bound by the same laws, as can be deduced from the law *Non ideo*, chapter *De liberali causa*.[19] From this it follows that, if someone is subject to the same kind of laws were to sell himself freely without these conditions in a place where these laws are not in force, the sale would be valid, because by natural law he can dispose of his own freedom; no wrong is done to a willing and consenting person. It follows that, if someone who in fact is subject to these [imperial] laws sells

12. On this legal action see Buckland, *The Roman Law of Slavery*, 656.

13. Cod. 7.18, 7.16.5 (*non ideo*), 7.8.3, 7.16.16, 7.9.3 (*servorum*).

14. Dig. 1.5.21.

15. Dig. 1.5.26.

16. Accursius, *Accursii Glossa in Digestum Vetus* in *Corpus Glossatorum Juris Civilis*, ed. Mario Viola (Turin: Officina Erasmiana, 1969), vol. 7; Dig. 5.1 at 10.

17. Antonino of Florence, *Summa Theologica* (Verona: Typographia Seminarii apud Augustinum Crattonium,1740) tit. 3, sec. V, col. 138.

18. Silvestro Mazzolini, *Summa Silvestrinae, pars secunda* (Venice: Dehuchini, 1587); "*De servitute et servo*" at 311–13. Angelus de Clavasio, *Summa de casibus conscientialibus, secunda pars* (Venice: Regazolae, 1578); "*servitus*" at 393–94.

19. Cod. 7.18, 7.16. 5 (*non ideo*).

another person into slavery without these conditions but does so in a place where these laws are not in force, such as [selling] an African in Africa, the contract would be valid and the person who has been sold would truly become a slave. It also follows that, if a person who is not subject to these laws sells himself without these conditions in a place where these kinds of laws are in force, the sale would be valid because these laws were enacted only for the freedom of those who are subject to them.

(21) One should know that the natural law allows parents to sell their children in cases of great need, as can also be seen in Exodus 21. Although, at one time, as Covarrubias comments in 3. *Variarum resolutionum cap.* 14, *n.* 4,[20] the law of Romulus allowed parents to sell their children three times if they happened to be freed twice and this even if the parents were not in need. Later, however, by Imperial Law, chapters 1 and 2, *De patribus qui filios suos distraxerunt*, it was sanctioned that this would not be allowed unless great poverty and hardship forced the parents [to sell their child], otherwise the alienation [of the child] was void.[21] (22) Moreover, whenever a fair price is offered to a buyer for a son or daughter that has been so sold or for some other price equivalent to that of another slave, the person who has been so sold shall not only be free but shall also be a freeborn (*ingenuus*) as if he had never fallen into slavery. What has been said of the sale should be understood to apply also to barter or to any other contract by which a child may be alienated to alleviate a very grave necessity of his parents. (23) Yet Covarrubias rightly asserts in the quoted text, as do many others, that if the father later obtains a fortune, he can be forced to redeem the child he has thus sold. (24) However, this power of the parents to sell their children in case of grave necessity is understood to apply only while the children are under the paternal power (*patria potestas*); when the children come of age, the parents are no longer allowed to do so, as states the gloss on law 2, codex *De patribus qui filios suos distraxerunt.*[22]

20. Diego de Covarrubias y Leyva, *Variarum Resolutiones* (Frankfurt: Lechler, 1578), book 3, chap. 14, n. 4 at 396.

21. Cod. 4.43.1, 4.43.2.

22. Accursius, *Glossa in Codicem* in *Corpus Glossatorum Juris Civilis*, ed. Mario Viola (Turin: Officina Erasmiana, 1968), vol. 10, 117b.

This is established by the Laws of Castile at law 8, title 17, part 4,[23] and corroborated by Aries Pinellus in the rubric codex *De bonis maternis,* page 2, n. 23.[24] (25) Now, if a child were to be married, even if by Common Law, he would not yet have left the paternal power; as it is the case in these kingdoms of [Portugal] and Castile, he could not be sold because doing so would be detrimental to his wife. Nowadays a father cannot sell his child if he is initiated in sacred orders, as Covarrubias says in the previous quotation, even if the sacred order were not to release him from paternal power. (26) Moreover, since by Imperial Law a child is not under the legal power of his mother, it cannot be sold by its mother by the same law, as the preceding quotation [of Covarrubias] affirms, as well as the preceding quotation from Aries Pinellus. (27) It is doubtful whether the father is allowed to sell the child, when the father's need is equal to or worse than that which would result from his great poverty and need, such as when he would be reduced to slavery or killed or mutilated, unless he sold his child. The cited gloss, which Covarrubias cited and others follow, argues the opposite because, as they say, the cited law concedes this faculty only in case of great poverty and need. However, I prefer the opinion of Pinellus, in the cited text at n. 27, where he says the opposite.[25] This law, therefore, must be extended by *epikeia* to cases where there is an equal or greater reason [that is, to justify the sale of the child], for if the legislator of that time had considered such cases, he would have mentioned them.[26] (28) I would like to remind the reader that the second law we have quoted is only in effect in places where Imperial Law is in effect, as we said earlier. For this reason, in Africa and other similar places, only natural law applies, unless some particular law happens to be in effect in that place. (29) Thus, in cases where the natural law permits a father

---

23. *Las Siete partidas del Sabio Rey don Alonso el nono, nuevamente glosadas por el Licenciado Gregorio López del Consejo Real de Indias de Su Magestad* (Salamanca: Andrea de Portonaris, 1555), partida 4, tit. 17, ley 8.

24. Ayres Pinel, *ad Constitutiones Cod. De Bonis Maternis* (Frankfurt: Bassaei, 1596), pt. 2, n. 22–23 at 144–45.

25. Pinel, *ad Constitutiones,* n. 27.

26. The Greek term ἐπιείκεια might be rendered as *equity.* On *epikeia* according to Molina, see Lorenzo Maniscalco, *Equity in Early Modern Legal Scholarship* (Leiden and Boston: Brill/Nijhoff, 2020), 146–47.

or a mother to sell their child out of necessity or for some other similar reason, and if the sale were to take place in a place where there is no particular law, the sale would be valid and the person sold would remain a true slave. Nor [in this case] would it [the child] be able to take advantage of the privilege [of regaining freedom], if the price paid or if a slave of equal value were offered, the freedom of the child would not be restored and he would not become again a freeborn, since this law was enacted in favor of the freedom of those who are subject to it [the law]. The same should be said if someone is sold in the same place, and who would be subject to the Imperial Law outside that place, for example, if one of us were forced by necessity to sell his child to the Africans.

(30) There is also a doubt as to what should be said about those among the Africans or Brazilians who are about to be killed and perhaps eaten by their own people, if they could be saved from death by offering a gift or a price. Could not someone who has made an agreement with them [that is, those who will be killed and eaten] to become his slaves and subject them to slavery once he has given [to the would-be killers] the offered gift or price? The answer to this doubt is that if such a person is to be killed justly by his own people, because he has been captured by them in a just war or because he was worthy of that punishment on account of a crime and, even if he were going to be eaten iniquitously, he could lawfully be bought and reduced to slavery.[27] Now, the reason for this is that there is no obligation, neither for the sake or justice nor by the law of charity to save this person from a just death. Not only is it fair, but it is also pious and utterly human to feel pity for those who are about to perish and to pay a price and exchange his death for slavery. And, even if he were bought cheaply, his slavery would have been just and no restitution would be owed to the slave because his slavery was not bought but rather was exchanged for his life. By contrast, in the case of the sellers, if the price [paid] was very cheap, an injustice would have been done [to them] unless perhaps the sellers tacitly wished to donate it [that is, to donate to the buyer the difference between the price paid and the just price of their slave].

27. *People* here refers to the ethnic group to which belong the two communities at war.

The case of a man who is about to be killed unjustly is more difficult, and a longer discussion is required. (31) First, if the person who offers the price is able to save the person by using force or in some other way without any cost or harm to himself, he would be bound by the law of charity, on pain of mortal guilt, to do so and leave the life [of the person unjustly condemned to death] intact along with his freedom. Second, if that wretched person has the means to pay the price safely later, he should be given a loan [of that amount]. Third, if he does not have this [money] and the price [for redeeming him] does not reach the value of perpetual slavery considering the usual cost of things in that region, it would be wrong to reduce him to perpetual slavery. There would be a duty to free him from death, so that he might be a slave temporarily until he repays the price and the lost profit, if the buyer has suffered such a loss or, if he has been freed, he should work until he repays that amount. Because in this eventuality, the full right to life would belong to him and not to those who would unjustly take it from him. Obviously, it is not his life that is being bought for this price [the price paid to free him], so that death (bought at whatever price) cannot be later converted into perpetual slavery as in the case where his life is about to be taken from him justly, which we discussed above. In this transaction, a price is offered so that no injustice may be done to him. For the same reason, it is only right to ask for the value of the price offered in the name of the other person's well-being but not for the value of his life, that is, the value he could ask for the commutation of his death. Fourth, if this price were equal to the price of slavery, he could buy that person for [the purpose of] perpetual slavery. This is what Navarrus says in the *Manual,* chapter 23, number 95.[28] The reasoning is that a person is not considered a pauper per se when he has the strength to work and is able to serve, so that we are not bound by the precept of almsgiving to freely give just any value for him in order to spare him from suffering extreme or grave necessity. For this reason, it is right to reach an agreement with such people so that they serve for as long as there is a need in order to compensate for the costs or lost

---

28. Martin Azpilcueta (Navarrus), *Enchiridion sive Manuale confessariorum et poenitentium* (Antwerp: Plantini, 1575) c. 23, n. 95 at 549.

profits, if there has been any, and also to reach an agreement so that they serve in perpetuity if the price is equal to that of perpetual slavery. This view is confirmed [by the fact that], when parents are in great need, it is licit to buy their children from them and they can sell them, so that they [the parents] are saved [from great need]. This is true not only when the children and parents are barbarians but also when both and the buyers are subject to the Imperial Laws, as stated in law 2, codex *De patribus, qui filius suos distraxerunt*.[29] Therefore, as far as natural law alone is concerned, it is licit to buy for a just price those who are in great need of receiving this amount because there is no greater reason for the slavery of their children than for themselves. If there were an objection to the third [argument], it would only be that by the precept of almsgiving we are obliged to give the price unconditionally to a person in extreme or grave need so that he can eliminate it. Since the precept of almsgiving obligates only out of charity and not out of justice, it follows that the person who makes a pact with someone in extreme need would be committing a mortal sin against charity but not against justice, so that he would be celebrating a valid contract by which he has bought a perpetual slave. For this reason, after slavery has already been agreed upon, the owner of the slave does not have a greater duty of almsgiving to give him [freedom] (especially if this status was not bought as a superfluous good) than he has a duty to grant freedom to any other of his slaves. Therefore, after agreeing to slavery for that reason [to save a person from dire need], he can possess him as a perpetual slave. If you add to this the fact that, according to the law of charity, it is the spiritual good that prevails over the physical good or freedom, you will see that (at least when the person in question is an infidel, whose being a slave contributes greatly to his spiritual health, insofar as he becomes a Christian and is baptized, also by reason of the education and the customs [thereby acquired], he will be much better off than if he remained in possession of his freedom), the precept of charity and almsgiving does not state that the price should be given unconditionally but rather as a compensation for perpetual slavery.[30]

29. Cod. 4.43.

30. That is, the person saved from unjust death should consider the money paid as ransom for the perpetual slavery that he will endure after being ransomed.

We believe that this assertion of Navarrus and our own is very true whenever slavery is conferred in such a way that the person bought acquires along with the life of the body the health of the soul, as it may often happen in Brazil or in Africa. Although we do not deny that this is true even when slavery does not contribute to the spiritual health of the person so bought—as the reasons provided seem to show—we do not doubt that Christians should be persuaded that, if the person who is to be sold is Christian, the price or loan should be given unconditionally, if he is not simply a pauper.[31] This is required by Christian charity, especially toward our fellow believers. We have never heard of a Christian who has sold his freedom or that of his children to other Christians to save himself from extreme or grave necessity, nor of anyone who, burdened by necessity and wishing to sell his child, would have found a Christian who would buy him; he may only find someone who would help him unconditionally or as a loan. A reason given by Navarrus also helps to confirm everything we have just discussed. [This reason], which cannot be disregarded, is that, although it is better in itself to pay the price unconditionally and out of almsgiving, even if the person who is saved from an unjust death is an infidel; in view of the state of men in this world and their avarice and infirmity, it is more pious to assert that in these cases of extreme necessity it is licit to pay the price for their freedom, otherwise there would rarely be people who would want to free someone unconditionally. The contrary opinion would easily give many the opportunity not to be saved from temporal death along with eternal death. Navarrus, in the text quoted, believes that those whose slavery would be bought in the manner explained enjoy the privilege of the second law of the codex *De patribus qui filios suos distraxerunt*, so that whenever these slaves, or anyone else, offered the owner a fair price or a slave of equal value, they would remain free and freeborn, by reason of the same argument that applies to the child sold by his father in extreme necessity to a father or to a free man without children, since he sells himself to escape the same necessity. But while this is to be accepted when both the buyer and the seller are subject to the Imperial Law, it is not to be accepted when they

---

31. That is, even if he can work.

are not, for this law was established only in favor of the freedom of those subject to the law and it would not be binding where men are not governed by Imperial Law.

(32) The fourth title is that of the condition of birth. Whoever is born to an enslaved mother is a slave, whether his father is free or not, whether he is born of a legitimate marriage or of fornication. This is stated in the law *Partum Codex de rei vindicatione sectio penultima*,[32] Institutions *De iure personarum sectio Sed et si quis*,[33] Institutions *De ingenuis*,[34] chapter *Unico de natis ex libero venire*,[35] and is generally in use in Spain. If, however, a mother is free at the time of conception or at the time of birth or any time in between, her child is born free. The reason is that, for the sake of freedom, the birth follows the womb (*partus sequitur ventrem*) that was free while the fetus was in it. This is stated in the paragraph *Sed et si quis*, Institutions *De ingenuis*, and scholars generally say this. However, when this [condition] has not been established for the sake of freedom, the very nature of the thing suggests that only the time of birth is to be considered, so long as this is in keeping with the laws and customs of the place [of birth]. But when there is another particular law or a custom that operates differently, so that the [condition of the] child follows [that of] the father or that to be a slave it is necessary for both parents to be slaves or something like that, then that law or custom would apply, as it is found in the chapter *Licet de coniugio servorum*[36] and as Panormitanus teaches in his commentary on it.[37] Nevertheless, the Imperial Law that we use in this country is particularly consistent with reason. First, because the mother is certain, while the father is uncertain. Second, because the mother's life is at risk at birth but the father's is not. Third, because, although the father has a greater role in procreation, the birth is yet in some way to a greater extent the fruit of the mother, and she is more involved in nourishing and raising

32. Cod. 3.32.27.

33. Inst. 1.4.

34. Inst. 1.4.

35. X.4.10.

36. X.4.9.

37. Nicolò dei Tedeschi (Panormitanus), *Abbatis Panormitani in Quartum Quintum Decretalium* (Lyon: Fratres Senetonios, 1547), 31B–32A.

her children, and she is more impeded than the father from serving her owner during the pregnancy and education of the child.[38]

38. Aquinas, in *ST* II-II q. 26 a. 10c. argues that "the father is principle in a more excellent way than the mother, because he is the active principle, while the mother is a passive and material principle" and continues (ad 1) "in the begetting of man, the mother supplies the formless matter of the body; and the latter receives its form through the formative power that is in the semen of the father. And though this power cannot create the rational soul, yet it disposes the matter of the body to receive that form" (trans. Fathers of the English Dominican Province). Scotists disagreed with the passive role assigned by Thomists to the mother, partly—it seems—because of disagreements on the status and role of Mary as the Mother of God. See Peter Tartaretus, *In Tertium Librum Sententiarum* (Venice: Inheritors of Simon Galignani de Karera, 1583), d. 4, a. 1 at 44–45.

Disputation 34

From what places slaves are imported by
the Portuguese and which among them may be
considered justly reduced to slavery by the
right of war by the Portuguese

Summary

1. The twelve islands of the Hesperides discovered by the Portuguese, given to them by right of occupation.

2. In their business with neighboring parts of Africa, for what prices and in what way do the Portuguese gather their slaves?

3. In what way are the slaves in those places reduced to slavery?

4. A very small theft (and also in num. 13) is punished by capital punishment or perpetual slavery.

5. The barbarous punishment of the children, relatives, or the family for the crime of the family's father.

6. The Portuguese do not inquire whether the slavery of those whom they acquire is just or unjust and how so.

7. When was the island of São Tomé discovered by the Portuguese?

8. On the Kingdom of Manicongo.

9. The Kingdom of Angola.

10. The captives of the Angolan War are slaves.

11. The fourfold condition of men [in a *mirinda*].

12. Daughters are sold in marriage in exchange for an ox or similar things.

13. [missing; see 4]

14. As a consequence of legal causes and legal inquiries, the *soba* punishes not only the guilty [*nocentes*] but also all his descendants.

15. The city of Sofala.

16. In the War of Sofala the captives are true slaves.

17. If they are subject to slavery, those who before or after or during the war have been acquired by the Portuguese only for the purpose of trading with these or other nations.

18. From what kingdoms may slaves be justly imported and what has to be said of the Japanese and Chinese (see num. 20).

19. The slaves acquired from the infidels and taken to Portugal reclaim their freedom for a small price.

20. [see 18]

(1) In order to understand this matter, one must know that the Portuguese, during their sailing expeditions in the year 1446, discovered the islands of Cape Verde, which the ancients called Promontorium Arsinarium.[1] In fact, these are the twelve islands they once called the Hesperides.[2] The main island is called Saint James, and there is the episcopal see, which is subordinate to the archbishopric of Lisbon, and the governor of the king of Portugal resides there. The Portuguese found these islands empty and began to colonize and inhabit them. (2) Therefore, based on the law of nations, the Portuguese, as the first occupiers, legitimately obtained ownership. From there they began to trade peacefully with their nearest neighbors in Africa, exporting their own merchandise to the Africans and also importing other merchandise from there. Those places in Africa (which begin in the realms of the Wolofs that were already infected by the Muslim sect, and which include many idolatrous territories) are called by us Upper Guinea and,

1. The Promontorium Arsinarium is in fact Cap Vert in modern-day Senegal (not an island). Here it is used to refer to the Cape Verde islands in the Atlantic, discovered possibly by 1446 in Alvise Cadamosto, Antonio da Noli, and Diogo Dias. See G. R. Crone, trans. and ed., *The Voyages of Cadamosto and Other Documents on Western Africa in the Second Half of the Fifteenth Century* (London: Hakluyt Society, 1937, reprint by Nendeln/Lichstentein: Kraus, 1967), 36–40.

2. It is not clear whether Molina had Pliny's *Natural History* in mind. In any case, the archipelago contains twelve islands.

in Portuguese, Guiné de riba.[3] Among the merchandise that the Portuguese brought back from these places are large amounts of gold, amber, and what we call *algalia* [civet oil], for these goods are in great demand because of their quality. There is also wax and an abundance of oxhide and a great number of slaves, and, although they are not bought so cheaply as the slaves from Lower Guinea, which we will discuss next, the merchants make such a great profit from them that on the Island of Cape Verde they pay a tax of a fourth part of [the value] of these slaves to the king or to the king's tax collectors, who are called Contratadores do Cabo Verde. They also pay a twentieth part of the remaining three quarters. After the complete distribution has been made, of those slaves who belong to the merchant that has arrived in Portugal, he [the merchant] pays first a tenth of [the value of] those [slaves] that have arrived safely, which they call the tithe, and of the remaining slaves he pays a *sisa*, that is, a tenth, unless he imports some for his own service.[4] And of those that he brought for his own service, he pays a tenth (unless the owner is exempt from taxes, such as the clergy) but not the *sisa*. The contractors enjoy the profitable privilege that, for each slave they export to Portugal, they only pay a *sisa* of three hundred bronze coins, which they call reis. It is not for me to explore whether they really pay the tithe at all. On the other hand, when they export slaves from these islands to places other than Portugal, they must pay ten gold coins for each slave so exported. However, when slaves are imported into Portugal from rivers and places in Africa rather than into the islands, a quarter [of the tax] of the slaves that arrive safely is paid as well as an additional twentieth part of the remainder. But those imported for service in a household are exempted from paying the *sisa*.

3. Upper Guinea refers to areas encompassing present-day Côte d'Ivoire, Liberia, Sierra Leone, Guinea, Guinea-Bissau, and Senegal. Apparently, due to winds and currents, it was easier to sail back to Europe from there, as opposed to the route from Lower Guinea, which stretches as far as Gabon and the island of São Tomé, where currents and winds favored westbound voyages. See J. D. Fage, "Upper and Lower Guinea," in *c. 1050–c. 1600*, vol. 3 of *The Cambridge History of Africa,* ed J. D. Fage and Roland Oliver (Cambridge: Cambridge University Press, 1977), 481 sq. See also David Eltis and David Richardson, *Atlas of the Transatlantic Slave Trade* (New Haven/London: Yale University Press, 2015), 96.

4. *Sisa* is a type of value-added tax.

(3) Now, the title by which these slaves are reduced to slavery by the Portuguese is not any right of war that the Portuguese have with these nations but only a purchase or barter of merchandise. For this reason, according to what we have discussed in the previous disputation, for the Portuguese to own them by a title of sale or barter, it is necessary that they [initially] be reduced to slavery by some other title unless one of them happens to be bought by a Portuguese to save him from a just or unjust death, which we have already discussed in the previous disputation.

However, after careful investigation, I will say a few things I have been able to find out about it. In our time, slaves of this type (with very rare exceptions) are not imported by the Portuguese for ridiculous prices, for a red cap or other small gifts or offerings of little value, as many have written. Rather, I hear that an investigation is being conducted in Cape Verde to see whether we have committed any wrong against the infidels, firstly, because this is required by good governance and, secondly, so as not to give the infidels an opportunity to kill those of us who live among them and to exclude us from trade, which they would easily do if they suspected such a thing, because, even if they are not as intelligent as our people, they are suspicious of us. Now, the titles by which the slaves are said to have been reduced to slavery before being sold by us are the following.

Among them [the Africans], it is rare to find powerful kings who have many subjects under them but, instead, they are divided among kinglets, dukes, and other such lords. Since ancient times, even before our people arrived there, there have been wars among them, and it is said that these peoples would fight with each other, harming each other by all means regardless of whether they are backed by right or justice. In this way, many people who were under one lord were captured by those who were under another lord and reduced to slavery, and many of them were sold to the Portuguese. They also say that, when the Portuguese ships arrived at certain places or rivers, the Africans would pillage the bordering towns more severely so that they would have captives to sell and trade for merchandise. Also, some of the Portuguese who live among these Africans conduct trade and they are called *tangosmãos*.[5] When some of the Portuguese ships arrive at a place, they enter the interior regions with some of the Africans and bring with them merchandise that they exchange in their markets or in the town square (*forum*) where they trade slaves who have been similarly captured, and they take them tied up for everyone to see to the ships and sell them to the ship merchants. It is also reported that in these places, under a certain tree and under the leadership of the lord and with the vote of the elders by simple majority, the subjects are judged, and some are condemned to perpetual slavery instead of natural death, while others are punished with death. (4) They punish the most trivial theft, even of one hen or some other small thing, with capital punishment or perpetual slavery. I was told that a certain king-let ordered his own child to be sold into slavery to the Portuguese as punishment for having been caught in petty theft. (5) For this reason, theft is extremely rare among them. It is said that their barbarity is so great that sometimes all the descendants, not only the children but also their brothers, are ordered to be killed or reduced to slavery for the sin of the father. If the prince is angry with one of them, he can easily order him to be killed or subjected to slavery, even the entire family.

(6) The Portuguese do not care at all about the title by which those who are sold in exchange for merchandise are reduced to slavery by their own people or by their enemies. Instead, they buy all the slaves that are brought to them as long as they like the price per head. In fact, they say that, if they wanted to inquire about this title, they could not find it out for certain. The Africans would not tolerate this [being asked about the origin of the slaves] any more than a seller of any merchandise among us would tolerate being interrogated about the title by the person who bought it. After all, as far as I have been able to understand from the merchants who buy slaves in Africa in this way and import them from there to here (those with whom I have spoken, and none of them disagree with what I have expressed here), they care for nothing

5. *Tangosmãos* are "Iberian or Capeverdean merchants who spent considerable time in Upper Guinea—and claimed to be exempt from paying taxes on slaves, since they had already paid very high taxes to the Portuguese crown upon departing the Upper Guinea coast." David Wheat, *Atlantic Africa and the Spanish Caribbean, 1570–1640* (Williamsburg: University of North Carolina Press 2016), 104.

in this business but their own profit and convenience. They are astonished if anyone wishes to express misgivings, and they think that the business with the Africans they import has been conducted correctly since, after buying them in this way, they [the slaves] are, as they claim, brought to the faith, and especially because they would lead a much better life among us as far as their bodies are concerned since they were naked among their own people and fed on meager food. When these merchants are asked whether there are sometimes slaves sold by Africans and brought to the ships who are either suspected or certain to have been stolen from their villages, they answer that it happens sometimes, though not so often. When they are asked again how they can buy them in good conscience, knowing that they were stolen and not legitimately reduced to slavery, some say that they do it because these slaves would be killed immediately by those who stole them if they were not bought, so that no one would know of their crime and so that their own people would not kill them [the African enslavers] for this crime. Others say that many do not dare to buy them in such a way [that is, by finding out the origin of the slave] because, if the matter were to come to light, the merchants themselves would be in danger. This is because the Africans impose a law on the merchants that they may not sell to anyone privately and that there must be an African elder present at the same time who can act as an interpreter and also to decide whether the slave has been stolen [and declare], "I have found that those slaves, too, are being bought."[6] And when sometimes these [slaves] are not bought, the merchants rarely fail to do so out of conscience but rather to escape the punishment and indignation of the Africans.

Among the Africans of Upper Guinea with whom the Portuguese conduct trade, they say that there are very few who eat human flesh. They also say that in previous years a certain queen went up there with a great army and subjugated many and that the food of the soldiers

---

6. This passage is juridically problematical because reselling or purchasing stolen goods is disallowed. Molina, talking to the merchants, has found that this is, however, common practice. In rare cases, the Portuguese merchants refrain from buying persons whose freedom had been stolen, not because of any kind of qualm of conscience, but simply because they fear legal sanctions or damage to their reputation. We are grateful to Wim Decock for his help interpreting this passage.

consisted largely of Africans whom they conquered and killed in order to eat their flesh.[7]

Up to this point we have explained the titles and ways by which Portuguese merchants import slaves. As for the business itself and its titles I see that the bishop of Cape Verde or the other priests who live there or even in this kingdom have no misgivings and instead they absolve the merchants and those who are called *tangosmãos*. Nor do I believe that the penitents confess these things or that any doubt moves them to confession or that the confessors even ask. Yet, if in these places the bishop or the royal governor sometimes punishes the *tangosmãos*, it is somehow only because they have not come to confession and communion for an entire year or because they have been in concubinage with an infidel (which is punished in that place) or because of some other excess and not because they have devoted themselves to this business. What is thought about these titles and this business will be discussed in the following disputation. Here we only report the facts.

(7) As the Portuguese advanced with their ships, in 1473 they discovered to the south of the equator the equally [to Cape Verde] uninhabited island of São Tomé, which they, as first occupants, began to licitly cultivate and inhabit according to the law of nations. Today there is another bishopric, which is subordinate to the archbishopric of Lisbon. From there, the Portuguese with their ships began to trade with neighboring African kingdoms and regions. All these territories are called Lower Guinea, which the Portuguese call "Guiné devaxo."[8] At this point, we need to talk mainly about two of the kingdoms with which trade was conducted.

(8) First, there is the Kingdom of Manicongo, which received with

7. This was Queen Macarico of the Mane People (who were also called Sumbas). See Walter Rodney, "A Reconsideration of the Mane Invasions of Sierra Leone," *The Journal of African History*, 8 (1967): 219–46, with references to cannibalism on 223. The main source for the story of this queen is André Alvares de Almada, *Tratado breve dos rios de Guine' do Cabo Verde* (Porto: Diogo Köpke/Typographia Commercial Portuense, 1841, originally from c. 1594). Mane cannibalism is discussed in chap. 12, 86. There is an English typewritten translation of the text: Avelino Texeira da Mota (edition and notes), P. E. H. Hair and Jean Boulègue (translation and notes), *Brief Treatise on the Rivers of Guinea* (Liverpool: University of Liverpool, 1984).

8. *De abaixo* in modern Portuguese.

its king the [Catholic] faith many years ago and is spiritually subject to the bishopric of the island of São Tomé.[9] In this kingdom, since all are Christians, no slaves are imported nor are they reduced to slavery on account of their crimes, but rather they are punished with other punishments by their king, although I have heard that in the past, when there was a rebellion to replace the deceased king, many were reduced to slavery by the victor. However, the Portuguese who inhabit this kingdom (who are called *pombeiros* here and in Upper Guinea *tangosmãos*) roam in company of Africans in inland areas and territories of the infidel, and with the merchandise imported from Portugal they buy great quantities of slaves, which they bring tied up in public and sell to the Portuguese merchants who land there with their ships and merchandise.[10]

(9) The second is the Kingdom of Angola, as we call it, which is most distant place where this trade is conducted. I said "as we call it" because that province is very vast and its inhabitants have been given the name of *ambundos* and so the province itself is called Ambundia, which is divided into many other provinces, just as Italy and France are divided into many provinces.[11] It has many quasi-kings that are called *sobas*, and the part of the provinces that they individually rule are called *mirinda*.[12] One of these *sobas*, approximately eighty years ago and with the help of some Portuguese who came there from the

9. With Manicongo, Molina seems to refer to the Kingdom of Kongo, although Manikongo or Mwene Kongo was actually the title of the ruler of the Kingdom of Kongo. Perhaps Molina confused this term with Mbanza Kongo, now São Salvador do Congo in the north of present-day Angola.

10. Actually, the *pumbeiros* were African slaves working for the Portuguese in the slave markets in Kongo, while *tangosmãos* were Portuguese mostly working in Upper Guinea; see Linda M. Heywood, *Njinga of Angola, Africa's Warrior Queen* (Cambridge, Mass., Harvard University Press, 2017), 259.

11. The term *ambundos* refers to the inhabitants of the Kimbundu speaking region north of the Congo River. Cabaça (Kabasa) was close to the modern town of N'dalatango. See John K. Thornton, *A History of West Central Africa to 1850* (Cambridge: Cambridge University Press, 2020), 58, 77–78.

12. *Soba* means "chief" in Kimbundu. See Mariana P. Candido, *An African Slaving Port and the Atlantic World: Benguela and Its Hinterland* (Cambridge: Cambridge University Press, 2013), 35. The function of a *soba* was to rule almost autonomously over a *murinda*, a small territory encompassing towns and small villages; see Thornton,

Kingdom of Manicongo with the aim of conducting business, launched a war against the neighboring *sobas*, whom he subjugated and forced to pay tribute, allowing them to keep the territories they already had. In this way, he expanded his empire in an extraordinary way. And since this *soba* was called Angola Inene, that is, "the Great," the Portuguese called that region "the Kingdom of Angola," the capital of which is a city called Cabaça.[13]

The Portuguese are now at war with this king for the following reason. This king asked many times for priests to be sent from Portugal and from São Tomé, assuring them that he wished to become a Christian, and among these priests there were monks of the Order of Saint Bernard. In reality he sought trade with the Portuguese as well as their help, rather than his spiritual health, because he doubted that without priests the Portuguese would settle there; yet [his request] was unsuccessful. However, some priests were killed in that kingdom and others returned to Portugal, while chalices and sacred ornaments were later found in the possession of the *soba*. As time went by and they found themselves deprived of commerce with the Portuguese, many envoys were sent by the *soba* to John III, king of Portugal, asking for priests and insisting that he, along with his subjects, wanted to receive baptism and offering very rich mines of silver that they had in their kingdom, as well as slaves.

These envoys were kindly received by the Portuguese king and treated most sympathetically, yet about 1560, they were dismissed with a delegation of the most benign king, with which Paulo Dias de Novais and four of our Company [the Company of Jesus] were sent so as to fulfill his wishes.[14] Upon arrival, they found that Angola Inene had died

---

A History of West Central Africa, 56–57. The Kingdom of Ndongo included approximately 725 *murindas*.

13. This was Ngola Kiluanje (known as Ngola Inene, Ngola the Great, 1515–56). On the political structure of Kongo, see Linda M. Heywood and John K. Thornton, *Central Africans, Atlantic Creoles, and the Foundation of the Americas, 1585–1660* (Cambridge: Cambridge University Press, 2007), 57–60; on Ngola Kiluanje, see Heywood and Thornton, *Central Africans, Atlantic Creoles,* 77. One of Molina's possible sources may have been the letters of Jesuit Balthazar Barreira to Antonio Mascarenhas. The letters were published in Balthazar Tellez, *Chronica da Companhia de Iesu nos Reynos Do Portugal* (Lisbon: Craesbeeck, 1647), chap. 30 at 629–32.

14. Dias de Novais (1510–1589) is credited with having brought Angola under

and that his son Dambi Angola was ruling in his place.[15] He happily received them in his city and treated them well at first, but later, moved by greed, he seized the goods this legate and the other Portuguese had brought with them to exchange for slaves that he would send to Portugal, saying that he would pay for them [the goods] with slaves. He did this but in a deceitful way, because he took the slaves back under some pretext, not so much out of greed for slaves but rather to prevent their return to Portugal. Finally, he took away all their goods, so that many of the Portuguese died and others returned destitute to the ships and he held the legate and two of our fathers against their will and without any profit, hoping that in this way the Portuguese would keep the trade with their kingdom. The other two Jesuit fathers died soon after because of the inclement weather. In the end, few of the Portuguese returned to Portugal. Although the legate was unable to obtain the return of these two fathers and the other Portuguese by trying to tempt the king in various ways and although the Portuguese king interceded, they still managed to persuade the barbarian king to allow the legate and one of us to return, telling him that this would more easily achieve what he wished and wanted, since they would report to the Portuguese king on the whole matter and of the case of the father who was left there as a hostage. A few years later that father, called Francisco Gouveia, unjustly detained and suffering from the long exile exile, died.[16]

In 1574, Paulo Dias de Novais obtained [the right to launch] an expedition from King Sebastian to avenge the injustice done to the Kingdom of Portugal that the African king had inflicted. The fame that existed at that time and that continued to grow was that there were many silver mines in that kingdom, which contributed to harming [the expedition]. I saw the instruction that was given to the admiral of the fleet after long discussions with those who in the Portuguese kingdom

---

permanent Portuguese dominion in 1575; see Heywood and Thornton, *Central Africans, Atlantic Creoles,* 82 sq.

15. Dias de Novais might have met Ndambi A Ngola in 1560, just one year before he died; see Heywood, *Njinga of Angola,* 263. More on Novais's involvement in the colonization of Angola in Heywood and Thornton, *Central Africans, Atlantic Creoles,* 82–90.

16. See Festo Mkenda, *Jesuits in Africa: A Historical Narrative from Ignatius of Loyola to Pedro Arrupe* (Leiden and Boston: Brill, 2022), 35.

were in charge of examining what concerned the conscience of the king.[17] It had been put together to exonerate him, prescribing how he should deal with that *soba* before declaring war, demanding, in the first place, compensation for the injustice done, etc. If this instruction, as it should, had been followed exactly, without greed blinding the commander and his soldiers or without their committing any transgression, it was clearly no more than could be desired for a war to be just. They also sent men of our Society [of Jesus] on that expedition who to this very day hear the confession of the commander and his soldiers. They preached to them and they converted many Africans to the faith, hoping that the whole kingdom would easily accept the faith if it were subjected to the rule of the Portuguese from the beginning.

From the reports of our men who went on that expedition, I learned that the governor, after landing there, had established his headquarters in the coastal part of the entrance to the kingdom, which is called Loanda. After it was discovered that Dambi Angola had died and that Quilonge Angola,[18] the great-grandson of Angola Inene, was reigning, they sent him a great gift that was meant to be given to his grandfather, Dambi Angola,[19] with an answer to what had been asked by the king of Portugal. With this and other gifts and favors, friendship and trade began with him, also to help him in the wars that he waged against the neighboring *sobas*. The friendship and trade between them lasted more than four years, without any injustice done to him or his people. On the contrary, they did them many favors and services. However, at the end of this time, when this barbarian saw the great abundance of merchandise that had been brought to his royal city by the thirteen or fourteen ships that had landed there and that there were thirty or forty Portuguese on each [ship] who were doing their own business or that of others, out of greed for such great trade and fearing that he might not be able to

17. This charter can be found in "Carta de doação a Paulo Dias de Novais" (September 19, 1571), in *África Occidental (1570–1599)*, vol. 3 of *Monumenta Missionaria Africana*, ed. António Brásio (Lisbon: Agência Geral do Ultramar, 1953), 36–51.

18. Molina is referring to Ngola Kiluanje kia Ndambi who reigned from 1561 to 1575. For more on the early rulers of sixteenth-century Angola, see Heywood, *Njinga of Angola*, 18–24.

19. Ndambi was Kiluanje's father, not his grandfather.

overcome so many Portuguese all at once, he initiated wars in various locations with which he divided them [the Portuguese] and ordered all of them to be killed on the same day, which actually happened.[20] Pretending that the Portuguese wanted to occupy his kingdom, he took possession of their merchandise and their other goods and he started a war against the Portuguese governor. The governor in turn, although he too had entered the interior of the region with the king's permission, was forced to burn the other goods that he had with him and to move himself and his people to a certain river from where he could wage war against the *soba* more easily. He made the neighboring *sobas* allies who feared that they would also lose their goods. He did this by protecting them and helping them against Angola [that is the ruler, N'gola] and the other *sobas* and by expanding their territories and by making them all vassals and tributaries of the Portuguese king, in which he happily succeeded. He fought against that enemy, who gathered nearly a million men against him, more than once, defeating them and conquering from them many places where the silver mines were located. Because of these and many other injustices that the barbarian king inflicted on our people, there is no doubt that the war was just, and, therefore, the enemies captured in it were justly reduced to slavery.

(11) But, since several other slaves, both from that kingdom and from the neighboring regions of the Kingdom of Manicongo and others, are exported, when they are bought or sold for merchandise and when others are donated by the *sobas* or paid by them as taxes, it is worth mentioning all that we have been able to find out about this question, partly through others but mainly from our fathers who live there, so that we may know more precisely whether these slaves are possessed justly or unjustly. This should also be examined because there may be some differences [between the reason for slavery in Manicongo] and the reason for slavery of the slaves that the Portuguese purchase in Upper Guinea and in the Cafreria[21]—which we will discuss later on—about which I do not have so much information, because none of our fathers reside there.

20. The attack on the Portuguese was carried out by a new ruler, Njinga Ngola Kilombo kia Kasenda (he ruled from 1575–92).

21. This refers to the coastal areas of what is now South Africa and Mozambique.

In each *mirinda* there are four types of men. The first are those called *mocotas*, who are the nobles and therefore freemen.[22] The second are the children of those born in that *mirinda*, who are called "children of the *mirinda*." They are farmers or craftsmen but they are also free.[23] The third class is that of those called *quisico*: these are serfs in the *mirinda* from time immemorial, who are bound to the estate, so that they pass on with all their descendants to the successor in the *mirinda*.[24] The *quisico* are the oldest group of these people to the point that there is no memory of their origins, only tradition. Since they have no form of writing, when they are asked about this point they tend to answer that it was the custom of their elders. Fourth, there are slaves called *mobicas*, who are the ones acquired by the *sobas* and other private persons as slaves and whom they dispose of at their will.[25] They do not only trade and sell them with the Portuguese in exchange for merchandise but much more, and from ancient times they have exchanged or sold them among themselves. They used to be traded among those peoples in the fairs and the public market, where they are sold and exchanged, and they usually are the price of many other things. (12) They also have the custom of selling their daughters for marriage in exchange for slaves, oxen, and such things, just as Laban sold his two daughters to the Patriarch Jacob to be his wives. Among them, the one who has the most slaves is considered the wealthiest because they [the slaves] are necessary for agriculture and for other businesses and services.[26] The children that the lords have with their female slaves are also slaves, and

22. *Makota*: noble man of Ndongo; see glossary in Heywood, *Njinga of Angola*, 259. On the social structure of the Kingdom of Ndongo, see also Heywood and Thornton, *Central Africans, Atlantic Creoles*, 72–79.

23. *Ana murinda*, which is the "taxable, but free population" of Ndongo; see Thornton, *A History of Central West Africa*, 71.

24. Actually *kijiko*, which are serf-like dependent people.

25. *Mubikas* were recently captured slaves who could be sold. See Thornton, *A History of Central West Africa*, 71.

26. According to Thornton, one reason for African slavery was that in sub-Saharan legal systems private land ownership was not allowed as a means of wealth accumulation, while the number of owned slaves did just that. See John K. Thornton, *Africa and Africans in the Making of the Atlantic World, 1400–1800* (Cambridge: Cambridge University Press, 1992), 102.

their father uses them for sale as if they were not his children. For this reason very often the family members of the *sobas* are slaves and are sold as such to the Portuguese and to others.

(13) The men of this fourth class are generally reduced to slavery in the wars that the *sobas* very often wage among themselves, without caring at all about the justice but only attempting to subject one another and in this way to expand their rule (*imperium*). Those who are captured in wars or raids are subjected to miserable slavery. I have been assured that, among the *sobas* who are in Angola, there are very frequent disputes and fights among those who are called *mochanos*. They submit their cause to the king, who delays the verdict of the case for as long as they offer him gifts and, when these cease because both adversaries are ruined, he replies that they should settle the matter by arms so that they wage war.

(14) In addition, many men of the first and second classes referred to above are reduced to slavery by their own *sobas* for crimes that are sometimes serious, sometimes minor, or even committed not by them but by one of their relatives, even without their knowledge and sometimes only on the basis of circumstantial evidence, accusations, and suspicions, whether true or fabricated by the *soba*.

First, if the *soba* has the slightest indication that someone is plotting to kill him, or is plotting against him, or is helping his enemies or anything like that, he may kill him or reduce him to slavery, taking all his goods and not only despoiling the suspect person but all of his relatives and anyone who is related to him. The rulings of the *soba* are enforced without needing any further inquiry or judgment. If one of the subjects discovers that the truth contradicts the *soba*, he is immediately reduced to slavery or killed, along with all of his relatives, while a single witness is deemed sufficient to convict anyone for the imputed crime. And it cannot be regarded but as wicked not only to kill someone or reduce him to slavery or deprive him of all his goods because of suspicions and indications, but it is even much worse to do the same to his innocent relatives and their kin even if the crime of the person is evident and these penalties would have been justly imposed on him. It is also said that in order to challenge the *soba*'s judgment it [the opposition] of the entire *mirinda* is needed or at least of its majority. For if a private man pretends to challenge the judgment [of the *soba*], he and all his relatives and their relatives will be guilty of lèse-majesté, and they will have to be killed or made slaves and have all their property confiscated. All of this and similar things are reported by the Portuguese soldiers and merchants who live there for their profit. Some of these *sobas*, who owe obedience to the king of Portugal, share these slaves and goods with the Portuguese. And the members of the religious orders cannot convince them otherwise, because the Portuguese allege to them that this custom of their homeland is not wicked but necessary because of the nature of the region (*regionis qualitate*). I have been told that when a *soba* must be condemned or punished by the Portuguese governor for committing a crime, it must be done according to the local custom before the army after all the *sobas* have been summoned along with their people and then the case against the accused is presented in the presence of the designated judges. And if, according to the custom of that region, he is deemed worthy of death and if he must be punished as being guilty of lèse-majesté, not only he himself is killed but all of his soldiers, even if they are nobles or children of the *mirinda*, and they kill many of them and the rest are reduced to slavery. They also rush to the house of that *soba* and tear it down, reducing to slavery all his relatives and even the women and children, miserably enslaving many innocents, and consequently, the Portuguese become richer with slaves and with the possessions of the innocent because of the fault of one criminal.

Among several other examples that have been reported to me of many people being unjustly reduced to slavery in these places, I will mention the following. One of these *sobas* sent a child as a gift [to the Portuguese] in the presence of one of our fathers. When one of the fathers asked him if he really was a slave and what the cause of his slavery was, he replied that one of his brothers had stared at one of the *soba's* women. For that reason he, along with all of his relatives, were stripped of all of their possessions as guilty of lèse-majesté and all of them were reduced to slavery, so that a child of noble descent was re-duced to slavery for the slightest transgression of one of his brothers, without any fault of his own. Then the father saw to it that the child's freedom was restored.

Only the king of Angola has peacocks, and he has them in great numbers. He issued a law: if someone were to take a feather from [the peacocks], he and his relatives would lose all their property and they would either be killed or be enslaved. He also issued another [law]: if someone were to hang gourds from the palm trees so that the wine from those palm trees drops into them, he and his relatives shall lose all their property and they should either be killed or be enslaved.[27] He has similar laws full of greed, cruelty, and injustice that deprive many innocent people of their goods because of insignificant transgressions of others, and they are either killed or unjustly enslaved. It would take a long time to list other examples of how many have been unjustly enslaved.

If a deceased person has left a debt, the *soba* will take all of his children as prisoners even if the debt is small and the children are of much greater value. Even in times of peace, men from one *mirinda* often kidnap those from another *mirinda*, selling them into slavery. It has even been reported that on a river that flows through the territory of enemies of one lord, business is done only at night and that the Africans bring prisoners during nighttime to sell them to the ships. This business is highly suspicious, as the Africans could easily transport men stolen from their own village or from someone else's. It has also been reported that the lords of the *mirindas* have sent people elsewhere to lie in wait to kidnap the prisoners [of another tribe] and sell them to Portuguese merchants. It has also been reported that, if a father is inflamed with anger toward his child or one of his wives for an insignificant reason, that this would be enough for him to sell the child or the wife. Sometimes he sells his child or his wife for no other reason than his desire to possess a small bell or a mirror or something else with which the Portuguese trade. Finally, it has been reported that in Lower Guinea many [people] eat human flesh, and it often happens that when a slave is offered for sale to a merchant and the merchant does not offer a price for the slave high enough to equal the profit that is usually made from [the sale of] flesh in the marketplace, then it would be better to kill the wretched slave than to sell him alive.[28] Such is the cruelty and

27. Gourds were attached to palm trees to collect the sap from which palm wine was made.

28. As early as 1580 trade in human flesh was reported by the Dominican João

barbarism of these people. The Portuguese merchants (whether those who dock their ships in different places to do business or those called *pombeiros* who go into the inner regions in search of goods or other inhabitants of the realms of Angola or Manicongo) do not care about the titles [under which these persons have been enslaved] nor do they ask how they were enslaved, when they were sold, or whether they have already been reduced [to slavery]; they take all the slaves without distinction as long as a price is agreed upon. Neither the bishop of São Tomé nor the secular priests who live in these places raise any concerns about what has been said about Upper Guinea. From Angola and other places in Lower Guinea entire droves of slaves are sent every year not only to the Portuguese kingdom but also to regions in Brazil where they are needed to harvest sugarcane and to produce sugar. [They are also shipped] to various other places in the New World for various kinds of labor but often also for [labor] in gold or silver mines. Although just as many or even more [people] die and are killed in wars every year, the people in those regions multiply because they have many wives and the land is humid and hot. [They multiply so much] that many more people remain in those areas, even though it is known that many more women live there than men because many die in wars every year.

The slaves from Lower Guinea are first shipped to the island of São Tomé unless the merchants agree to transport them from the realm of Angola [directly] to Brazil. In that case 3,000 copper coins, known as reis, are paid for each slave. Of those who are shipped to São Tomé, a quarter of the profit is paid to the king or the hirer and an additional twentieth of the remaining slaves, unless the merchants conduct their business using the king's ships or those of the tax collectors.[29] In that case they pay half the price of [the slaves]. When the slaves are shipped from São Tomé to Portugal, then the *sisa* is paid only for them, such as has been said above concerning the slaves from Upper Guinea. If the hirers of royal profits were to ship them [to Portugal], they would receive 300 reis for each slave.

---

dos Santos, who lived in Southeast Africa from 1586 to 1597. João dos Santos, *Ethiopia Oriental* (Evora: Manoel da Lira, 1609), 65.

29. The reference seems to be to persons who purchased from the crown the right to collect royal taxes called *arrendadores* in Spanish.

(15) In 1501, Portuguese ships reached Sofala after passing the Cape of Good Hope.[30] After establishing a fortress there, they began to trade with the neighboring kingdoms. Apart from gold and other merchandise, they also brought strong slaves of large complexion [size], who are called *cafres*, who were shipped to India and then, in no small part, to Portugal on Indian ships. They used to be shipped mostly after they were bought and then traded for other merchandise. In 1569 King Sebastian sent the most noble and vigorous commander, Francisco Barreto, who shortly before had been governor in eastern India and who achieved much with strength and fortune.[31] [He was sent] to justly punish King Munhumutapa, a neighbor of Sofala, after he had followed the ill-willed advice of some Muslims and unjustly and disgracefully, from the point of view of our Christian religion, killed a father of our Society, the son of the duke of Sortelha, Gonçalo da Silveira.[32] After this father, who shortly before had been provincial [of the order] in India, had made an agreement with this king to spread the word of God in this kingdom and to convert thousands to the [Catholic] faith, some Muslims instilled in the king vain and childish fears that this father was a poisoner and that, unless he were killed, the king would lose his kingdom because of the poison and the enchantments. For this reason, [Munhumutapa] ordered the father to be killed; [the father] already knew this and expected to be killed and at the same time [the king] demolished and destroyed existing churches. Mainly to punish these aggressions and without much hope of taking possession of the rich gold mines that exist in that kingdom, Francisco Barreto (accompanied by some of ours [Jesuit fathers]) left with instructions that were very similar to those we have spoken of before and that we could inspect ourselves. Even though he [Barreto] and his successor waged war for some years against that king and with some others who were his followers, whom it was first necessary to defeat, they fought many brave [battles], and eventually many of our men, along with Francisco Barreto, were gradually consumed by the poison of those men, by war and

30. Sofala is located in present-day Mozambique.

31. For more on the Portuguese presence in southeastern Africa, see Mkenda, *Jesuits in Africa*, 32–34.

32. *Mwenemutapa* in the Shona language.

disease, and so the war stopped. A large number of the soldiers who remained unharmed departed for India.

(16) About the slaves who were captured by the right of war, the same has to be said as we said about the slaves who were captured by the Portuguese right of war in the Kingdom of Angola. It has just been said that there is no doubt that our people reduced them to slavery on the basis of a just title. It has been reported that some of those kings gave us other reasons for a just war when they invaded and plundered our fortresses. If some of these men were captured by Francisco Barreto either before or after the war in an otherwise just war, then the same can be concluded [that is, that the slavery is just].

(17) As for the slaves who were acquired by the Portuguese before, after, or during the war only through commerce with them or with other nations, which in those entire regions of Africa are called Cafreria, I think that almost the same titles apply by which they are reduced to slavery and also with regard to the way in which the Portuguese conduct their business, which has been spoken of above with regard to the slaves of Upper Guinea. It has also been reported that in times of famine or even when oppressed by large debts among their people, some are forced to sell their children to alleviate their hardship. It is also said that among these Africans there are nations that eat human flesh. Furthermore, all these Africans sell slaves to the Portuguese as well as to the Muslims who live among them and who transport these slaves along with other merchandise to other Muslims to sell them as slaves.

(18) With regard to Asia: The Portuguese transport from India various kinds of slaves according to the variety of nations with which they are engaged in war or commerce. Of this I will speak only summarily. When the slaves come from kingdoms against which the Portuguese are waging a just war, we should not recoil from saying that they were justly reduced to slavery. Those who come from the Kingdom of Calicut, among others, are of this type.[33] After we [the Jesuits] arrived in India, from the beginning the king there was extremely hostile to us and the Portuguese were always at war with him. I hear, however, that in

33. The Kingdom of Calicut (Kozhikode) was situated on the coast of modern-day Kerala, India. The war started in 1500 with Pedro Alvares Cabral's attempt to set up a factory.

1586 peace was made with him.[34] Of this type [that is, captured in a just war] are also the slaves who come from the Golden Chersonese, that is, from the island of Sumatra and from the region of Malacca, which is adjacent to this island. All this was once called the Golden Chersonese. It is said that the island that now is called Sumatra was once connected to the continent by a tongue of land or an isthmus, which was separated by the rising sea, leaving behind a peninsula. Our people call the inhabitants of Sumatra "Dachens,"[35] the others "Malayans." We must also add those who live on the island of Java and whom our people call "Jaos." With all these [peoples] the Portuguese almost always waged a just war. All these [peoples] in their appearance and stature are between the Indians and the Ethiopians, who live in Africa. The same has to be said of the rest of the slaves of the kingdoms against which the Portuguese waged just wars, when they were reduced to slavery and for whom no pre-established rule [as to whether these wars were just or unjust] may be provided. I have said that many call the island of Sumatra the Golden Chersonese, while others seem to think more correctly that the island of Ceylon [Sri Lanka] is the Golden Chersonese.

Many slaves, however, are transported from provinces against which the Portuguese are not at war, such as Cambay, Pegu, China, Japan, and others. Although it is said that in the Kingdom of Cambay and other [provinces] of India famine is frequent and that in such circumstances people not only sell their children or even themselves for a paltry price, [it is also reported] that, even when there is no famine, many steal their children and sell them not only to us but also to the infidels.[36] (19) This

34. This was an agreement between Gaspar Fagundes and the Zamorin (the local authority) to help him against the Kunjali (the Zamorin's Muslim admirals who had turned against him). See R. R. S. Chauhan, "Kunjali's Naval Challenge to the Portuguese" in *Essays in Goan History*, ed. Teotonio R. de Souza (New Delhi: Concept, 2002), 32.

35. This refers to the inhabitants of the Aceh sultanate in modern-day Indonesia.

36. "The infidel" here refers to the Hanthawaddy Kingdom in present-day Myanmar. See Manuel de Abreu Mousinho, *Breve Discurso en que se cuenta la conquista del Reyno de Pegu* (Lisbon: Craesbeeck, 1617). For a more general discussion, see also Paulo Jorge de Sousa Pinto, *The Portuguese and the Straits of Melaka, 1575–1619: Power, Trade and Diplomacy* (Singapore: NUS Press, 2012). On the famine in India and Portuguese relief efforts, see Anthony R. Disney, "Famine and Famine Relief in Portuguese

is despite the fact that not only the provincial council of India but also the royal laws of Portugal make sure that those infidels living under the jurisdiction of Portugal shall not possess this kind of slave and that those who arrive in our territories shall be freed upon payment of a small price, prudently fixed in view of the prevailing circumstances, so that they may diligently receive their freedom, and for this reason many would easily receive the Christian faith. But the Muslims who live in those regions are forbidden under severe punishment to transport or sell slaves because they use to blind [others] severely with the errors of their deviant sect. I do not know, however, whether the slaves of the kind that the Portuguese sell and transport have undergone the careful scrutiny [to determine] whether they have been licitly reduced to slavery. Nor [do I know] whether [the Portuguese] who bought them from an infidel investigated whether they had been legitimately subjected to slavery or whether they had been legitimately subjected at the time they were bought by the infidel.

(20) Moreover, although internal wars among Japanese princes are very frequent, one might doubt the justice of these wars because these infidels do not seem to care about the justice of beginning such wars. Rather the one who is more powerful or who has the greater hope of achieving victory attacks the other with the force of his weapons and tries to subject him. Assuming this, the one who defends himself against an unjust war considers it to be a just war. But one might assume and believe that the wars that the Christian Japanese princes are waging today against infidels are just, since the fathers of our Society preach to them and hear their confession, and they would not allow them to commit anything unjust against them [the enemies]. But I do not know whether the Portuguese merchants, when they purchased Japanese people as slaves and maids, took it upon themselves to examine whether they had been captured and enslaved in a just war or not.

As for the Chinese slaves, whom the Portuguese buy and transport, there is greater doubt as to whether they were ever reduced to slavery on account of a just title and by what right they could be justly

---

India in the Sixteenth and Early Seventeenth Centuries," *Studia* 49 (1989): 255–81, and his *The Portuguese in India and Other Studies, 1500–1700* (Routledge, 2018).

possessed by those under whose power they came, even if they were bought at a fair price. It is clear that the Chinese provinces enjoy permanent peace, since they only wage war against the Tartars who are far away from our commercial [routes]. It is also clear that these provinces are very prosperous and that they never suffer from famine, so that no Chinese could legitimately sell his own children due to the severe lack of [basic] needs. It is also clear that Chinese judges do not condemn any of their own [people] to permanent slavery unless they were to render services to their king for some purpose. From this it follows that among the just titles, which we have discussed in disputation 33, there is none by which these Chinese could be subjected to slavery unless perhaps some Chinese pirate from China had been captured by the Portuguese with his people, either with the consent of the Chinese or because he was angry with the Portuguese. I do not think this is credible, and it would not remove the doubts about the Chinese women who were brought to the Portuguese as captives.[37]

So as not to take up the discussion about the Chinese in the following disputation, I will say the following.

If, as has been reported, the origin of the slavery of the Chinese owned by our people is nothing more than theft, by which the Chinese steal from one another in order to sell [slaves] to foreigners, then surely none of them is legitimately possessed regardless of the amount of money for which he [the slave] was bought from the hands of a thief or from the hands of another seller under whose power he came. The reason for this is that ownership is never acquired by the purchase of a stolen thing, regardless of the person who acquires it and the price for which it was bought. Rather the ownership has to be restituted as soon as it is clear that it has been taken by theft unless he had possession in good faith for such a long time that it [restitution] has to prescribe.[38] Therefore, since freedom does not prescribe at any point in time, as is

---

37. On these see Lúcio de Souza, *The Portuguese Slave Trade in Early Modern Japan: Merchants, Jesuits and Japanese, Chinese, and Korean Slaves* (Leiden and Boston: Brill, 2019).

38. As to the origin of the concept of good faith in ancient Roman Law, it has been observed that "*bona fides* came to serve as a powerful quasi-ethical principle in the jurists' further development of contract law. *Bona fides* had become not just a

established by the last law of the Codex *De longi temporis praescripti-one, quae pro libertate* and the chapter *Usucapionem* from the law *De usucapionem*, as well as shown in law number 6, title 29, *partida* 3, of the laws of Castile.[39] Even if freedom were to prescribe according to our laws, the law cannot be imposed on another republic and its people, in which they [the laws] are not valid. Consequently, it must be said that, if these men were initially taken by theft, then they, as well as the offspring of the women who were initially subjected to slavery, are free and they cannot justly remain in slavery. They rather have to be restituted,[40] as will be discussed in the following disputation, because, although they are free, they were held captive either in good or in bad faith. For the same reason, the same must be said of anyone who has been subjected to slavery without a just title.

After I wrote this, I shared it with a father of our Society who has lived in China for a long time and who has traveled to the inner [regions of China], and he approved [my account].

---

reason for enforcement, but also an independent source of obligation." Bruce W. Frier, *A Casebook on the Roman Law of Contracts* (Oxford: Oxford University Press, 2021), 9.

39. Cod. 7.22., Inst. 2.6, *Siete partidas* (1555), vol. 2, partida 3, ley 6, at 166. According to Roman Law, the term *praescriptio* is designed to impose a limit on legal claims. A special case is the *praescriptio longi temporis*, usually ten or twenty years. See Adolf Berger, *Encyclopedic Dictionary of Roman Law* (Philadelphia: American Philosophical Society 1953), 645. The point here is that a legal claim for freedom is not limited in time.

40. Their freedom has to be restored.

Disputation 35

What to think of the Portuguese trade with slaves

Summary

1. Charles V gave the slaves of the New World freedom, prohibiting slavery henceforth.

2. Philip II excluded the children of the rebels in Granada from slavery.

3. When do merchants justly transport slaves to Portugal or purchase them?

4. Someone is justly bought if he has been subjected to slavery by a public authority for a sufficiently serious crime.

5. Can someone related to a criminal by blood or by family be reduced to slavery because of his [the criminal's] wrongdoings? (See also number 7)

6. What crime is enough to condemn someone to slavery?

7. [title is missing]

8. Merchants have a duty to inquire whether the slaves have been subjected due to crimes perpetrated by others.

9. When is it allowed to purchase infidels who offer themselves and their children: in case of grave scarcity [of food] or need?

10. Are debts a sufficient reason to sell their children?

11. If there is a rumor or a suspicion that some slaves are being sold unjustly or that children are being subjected [to slavery] for reasons other than famine or grave necessity, then the merchant must inquire into the cause.

12. Is the purchase of slaves for an insignificant thing or a small price just?

13. If outsiders cannot establish which of the two warring republics is waging a just war after conducting moral due diligence, then they are allowed to buy either movable things seized by soldiers in the war or captured [soldiers].[1] Which right applies when the purchasing persons come to know afterward that the war has been unjust?

14. Do soldiers who recapture movable goods that have been seized by the enemy have a duty to return them to their former owner?

15. When it is clear that two republics are fighting each other unjustly, do the captured [things] belong to the one who captured them and can an outsider buy them?

16. Those who purchase things, especially slaves, captured in war from one of the warring republics commit a mortal sin if they do not inquire about the justice of the war.

17. Wars among Africans are rarely seen as just.

18. On the injustice committed by the Portuguese who trade slaves in Africa. It is right to remedy this.

19. As long as these nations are infidel, slavery must be protected for the benefit of the faith transmitted to the slaves, as far as justice and neighborly love permit.

20. The difference between someone who believes that something probably belongs to him without being completely certain and someone who secretly seizes it from someone else who has begun to possess it in good faith and someone who takes it but doubts whether the thing sold or given was stolen.

21. If a merchant buys [a slave] while in invincible ignorance, [not knowing] that there is no just title to subject him to slavery and afterward expresses doubts, what are his obligations?[2]

---

1. The term Molina uses is *dilgentia* or *diligentia moralis*. This corresponds to a kind of due diligence that was usually required in commercial transactions, because seller and buyer must always be certain that the thing sold was in the legal possession of the seller.

2. Invincible ignorance morally excuses the agent insofar as this ignorance could not have been avoided, even after taking all the necessary precautions.

On this subject, there is nothing easier or more certain to say than that slaves who were originally reduced to slavery by any of the titles explained in disputation 33 may be lawfully imported and possessed. However, those who have not been thus subjected to slavery cannot be lawfully imported, nor can they be kept, even if they have been purchased at the appropriate price and even if they have been possessed in good faith for any length of time up to that day, as we have just demonstrated. However, the more general moral admonition is, as Aristotle prudently taught in book II, chapter 7, of the *Ethics*, the less useful and true it is with respect to completing particular actions. If someone were to carefully consider the things that are said to have provided a faithful history of the subject in the preceding disputation (and these do not contain all the abuses that can be recounted), one would easily understand that this subject is filled not only with scruples but also with many manifest dangers to their souls. I will try to say something in a specific way, even if reluctantly, and only to clear my conscience. Not that I dare to define such an important matter by myself or because I am so important that I would want everything to stand by my words and judgment on the subject. Acknowledging my own paucity, I rather wish to give advice to confessors and God-fearing people who are investigating this subject, especially since there is no lack of foreign writers of the sort who boldly condemn this commerce as a mortal sin.[3] If this disputation has any value, it is that it may contribute to the fact that those to whom the governance of this Portuguese kingdom is entrusted and whose task it is to examine all that concerns the king's conscience and who have the task of exonerating him—as well as those who hear the king's confessions (each and every one of whom along with the bishop of Cape Verde and the Island of São Tomé are undoubtedly bound to do so under the guilt of mortal sin, if, at the very least, the subject presents itself to them as doubtful)—will suggest to the king

3. The Portuguese slave trade had already been criticized by Spanish theologians such as the Dominican Tomás de Mercado, *Suma de tratos y contratos* (Salamanca, 1569), fol. 66v, who, while noting that "[t]he trade in black people in Cape Vert is, considered in itself, licit and just" adds that, given "the infamy that attaches to it and beyond the true reality of what is taking place, it is mortal sin, and the traders who export black people from there are in a bad [sinful] situation and great [moral] danger."

to have the matter carefully weighed and judged with the help of what the consciences of learned and God-fearing men demand. Having first made a diligent and certain investigation as to the titles and modes by which these people are in fact thus reduced to captivity and imported as captives, they may decide what is just and unjust and they may decide what needs to be done so that the conscience of the king may be safe as well as that of the merchants and of those who purchase slaves from them. (1) When doubts arose concerning the slaves of the New World, Charles V, in order to assuage his own conscience and that of his people, ordered an investigation of the matter, and he passed a law worthy of a Christian emperor that they should all be granted their freedom and that none should be subjected to slavery henceforth.[4] (2) When doubts began to arise concerning the innocent children of those who rebelled in the Kingdom of Granada and were justly made slaves, Philip II, his son, our most Catholic king, also passed a law that they should all be granted their freedom, although, as we have shown in disputation 33, in our opinion, he was not obliged to do so. Why then, I ask you, if the subject we are discussing would immediately appear to some to be difficult and full of dangers, and since there is no lack of writers who would condemn it as an unjust mortal guilt, and since today the consciences of many God-fearing men are pricked, why should it not, if the king orders it, be examined and stopped if it has been found out that something has been done unjustly and why should it not be approved with the mature judgment of a public authority if it has been done justly and lawfully? The result will be that rumors of injustice and scandal, if any, will cease and that the king will assuage his own conscience and that of his people and that no confessors or other learned and God-fearing men will trouble these merchants without cause or, if anything could be found worthy of being cancelled, after everything has come to light, that the merchants, blinded by greed, would not be able to defend themselves against the confessors and scholars by objecting that this business grants a spiritual good to the slaves and that they themselves were the first to engage in it and that neither the king

4. Apparently, Molina is referring to the *Leyes Nuevas* (new laws) from 1542, by which the indigenous population is granted a series of legal protections, among others against slavery.

nor the bishops of these regions could oppose this kind of business or cast doubts on it. All these things, if the matter itself is unjust, are of no weight or importance, so as to excuse them from mortal sin and the burden of restitution. I myself do not doubt that—if this matter had once been presented as doubtful to either Philip, our most Catholic king, or in their time to Manuel, John III, Sebastian, and Henry, the most Christian pious kings of Portugal, so that they would have perceived any danger of injustice in it—they would have immediately ordered it to be investigated and settled. However, since these things were done in maritime regions far away from Portugal and since they began gradually, the later kings did not discuss the matter, and perhaps it would not have been appropriate [for them to discuss] practices that were introduced by their predecessors when there was no doubt about these issues. Learned and God-fearing men have seldom reached the places where these things are done, and there are few among us who care about these issues and pay attention to them, and there are even fewer who either can or dare to suggest these issues to kings. It is no wonder that this matter has not reached the ears of the princes who, together with their people, were occupied with various other matters and that, even to this day, they have not taken counsel in this matter as they should.

We have brought up this subject not to define it completely but to shed some light on its complete definition, and we will try to separate what is certain from what is uncertain.

(3) Let this be the first conclusion: If the slaves captured in a war come from places where, as we have said in the previous disputation, there was a just war between them and the Portuguese and if they were imported from those places at a time when there was such a war, the merchants who import them from there need not make an inquiry if there is no plausible presumption to the contrary about one or more [slaves] and much less should an inquiry be made by those who buy them in this kingdom from merchants or from any other person or buy them under any other title. The same is true when the war is over and there is no rumor or suspicion that anyone has been unjustly reduced to slavery from any of these places. The first part is proved because, since the war of the Portuguese in these places is just and since it can be

assumed that the seller is honest and sells what he owns or what he has the right to sell, unless other plausible conjectures to the contrary arise or deserve to be considered, then it must be assumed and presumed that all the slaves offered for sale have been reduced to slavery in a just war, unless probable conjectures arise about one or the other [slave] in particular that they have been subjected to slavery unjustly. This is confirmed because, as in any other transaction an inquiry as to whether the item sold is legitimately sold would be overly scrupulous and super-fluous unless a legitimate reason for supposing or fearing the contrary were to present itself, so also in this transaction an inquiry as to wheth-er a slave sold has been legitimately reduced to slavery would be super-fluous and overly scrupulous when there is no rumor to the contrary and if no legitimate reason for doubt arises. The second part, that those who buy slaves in this way from the merchants of this kingdom are much less obliged to make inquiries, is well known, either because the same or a better reason supports them or because the distance is too great for them to be able to make, if they so wished, any fruitful inquiry about each and every [slave] in particular or because it is the duty of the king and the king's ministers to be vigilant and to discuss whether the slaves that are imported into this kingdom, especially from places with which it has commercial relations, have been legitimately subjected to slavery. For the third part we have the same reason: When the war is over, and there is no rumor, etc. [that slaves were unjustly taken]. It is proved because the same reasons apply, and it is presumed that slaves of this kind either belong to those who were captured in the war or were born to women who were captured in the war or were reduced to slavery by some other just title. This conclusion shows that there is no need to inquire whether Turks, Moors, and their children who are offered for sale have been legitimately reduced to slavery, if there is no legitimate reason to doubt whether anyone in particular is free. There have always been legitimate wars between Christians and these nations.

(4) The second conclusion is that in both Guineas, as in any other place, it is lawful to buy someone who has been reduced to slavery for a crime that the public authority of the government in that place considers sufficient for that punishment. (5) However, it is not lawful to reduce someone's wife to slavery for the crime of her husband, nor

someone's brother or other close relatives, nor his more distant relatives, nor even his children, neither those who are legally independent nor those who are under the authority of their father, unless the crime was so terrible and infamous that in the judgment of prudent people it has been decided that their children also must be punished with slavery for the good of the republic and as an example to others.[5] Even in this case it would be better to punish him in those children who originated from the crime [i.e., in a sexual crime] than in the other children, even though it is very rare that a crime of the father can be justly punished with the slavery of his children. To put it simply, a child who has been reduced to slavery in those places only because of the crime of his father cannot be bought.

(6) The first part is clear from what has already been said in disputation 33. However, we can give this rule: a crime that, in the judgment of a prudent man, we would punish by sending the criminal to row on a galley perpetually, but also a crime that we deem worthy of a somewhat lesser punishment, should be judged sufficient for someone to be justly condemned to perpetual slavery. This is proved by the fact that this punishment [rowing at the galleys] is a much harsher punishment [than the other punishments among us], and the slavery of those rowing in galleys is much more pitiful than is the slavery of common slaves. Therefore, the adultery of a wife of an African, even if he has many wives, would be enough to condemn her and her adulterous partner to perpetual slavery. It is the same with violence against a woman's chastity, and with the theft of something that is famous in a region for its quality, and with other crimes of this nature. But a petty theft, such as the theft of a hen, would not be sufficient for this, unless the experience was acquired that such a punishment would deter people from stealing and unless these very petty thefts were severely punished, the number of thefts would increase to the detriment of the republic. Similarly, we do not condemn the fact that in the army minor infractions are punished with death or with galley slavery, because military discipline and the common good of the army require it. The same is true when the common good of the republic requires that petty thefts be severely punished; this punishment

5. The notion of a legally independent person is an adaptation of the concept of being *sui iuris* from Roman Law.

would be allowed, especially if everyone knew beforehand that this punishment would be inflicted on anyone who committed this crime. We have learned from experience that Africans are inclined to the vice of theft, yet we hear how rare theft is in the places from which they are imported, although there is far less custody of these things among them than among us. Just as we cannot easily affirm that these people in these places have been justly condemned to slavery for petty theft, neither should we fear to reject [this practice]. Consequently, if those among them who are condemned to perpetual slavery because of petty theft or who will be killed by their own people unless they are bought by the Portuguese, then they may lawfully be bought, because they would thus be saved from death; [a death] that would not be inflicted without sufficient guilt considering the customs of that region.

(7) The rest of the conclusion is clear from the fact that the very light of nature teaches that it is wrong to punish a completely innocent person for the transgression of another person, especially with so great a punishment as perpetual slavery, except perhaps [in the case of] a child, while it is still under his father's legal authority, the father is punished in the child as if it were a part of him, because the child has the closest connection with his father. Hence, an innocent child should not be punished except in the rarest cases when it is required by the greatest good of the republic. We do not know of a child who has ever been condemned to slavery in the whole of Canon Law and Civil Law, except only for one who is born of the crime of both of his parents who refuse to end a condemned or scandalous marriage in which the husband is an initiate in the sacred orders. Even in this case, the child is only condemned to serve the Church and no one else. (8) Since there is a rumor, and the merchants themselves admit it, that among the Africans the children, wives, and brothers of the delinquent are sometimes reduced to slavery for the crime of another person, even the most trivial one, the merchants, when selling them as slaves, must naturally ask and inquire whether these slaves have been condemned for the crime of another person and they must teach the Africans that neither the right of nature nor our most sacred law permits it and that they themselves cannot buy or possess these [slaves] with a clear conscience. They must also inquire whether a father sells his child or wife for a trivial offense

or without a just cause, for they acknowledge that the Africans often sell their own children and wives without a just cause, and sometimes it is merely because they desire to obtain a bell or some other merchandise from the Portuguese. Nor can the claim made by merchants [be accepted] who, in order to justify their own greed, say that the Africans would take offense if they were asked about the titles under which the slaves they sell to them were reduced to slavery and interrogate them in the way described scolding them about what is allowed and what is not. But no one takes offense because they are being taught the natural law, which they do not know and that they are being admonished to follow. Much less can we assume this of the Africans, who look up to the Portuguese. On the contrary, they will be edified by admiring our most sacred law and religion that prohibits this, and they will honor it. However, if merchants do not wish to inquire into the titles in the above fashion, whenever the Africans admit that they sell many slaves in this unjust manner, they should abstain altogether from trading in such slaves. If there is a suspicion that others are selling slaves that are not their own, one must abstain completely from doing business with them. A person who buys something like this from them is not called a possessor in good faith, but rather, in addition to the sin that he commits by buying from them, he is obligated to exercise due diligence afterward to know whether the thing was sold legitimately. Now, if there is no due diligence to find this out afterward and if the doubt remains whether it was sold legitimately, then the burden of restitution of a part of the value of the thing purchased would fall on this person in proportion to the amount of doubt that remains. In the situation discussed, restitution must be made to the slave, who is the one who possessed his freedom and about whom there is doubt as to whether it [freedom] was sold legitimately.

(9) The third conclusion: In places in India where there is severe famine among the infidel and in all similar places or situations, it is allowed to approach and purchase children from the infidel in exchange for food supplies or money and even to buy the parents who want to sell themselves as slaves. But it is wrong to deny them food supplies, if they offer a fair price, and to force them to sell their freedom, while it is right that if one offers freedom and another price and one cannot

help both, then the one who offers [in addition] his freedom should be preferred. It is also wrong to buy from the infidels children who are under the legal authority [of their parents] except in cases of greatest need and when there is no other way to help this person conveniently. Yet, if someone were to buy them without this necessity, he would be obliged to restore the freedom of the persons whose ownership he never obtained and [he should pay] additionally a price for all their services and benefits, which he has received from them. Yet, he could buy their parents without [having to prove] great necessity if they wished to sell themselves of their own accord. Children who are under the legal authority of their fathers, if they have already reached the age of legal responsibility and are capable of celebrating a contract, may be bought without them or their parents suffering grave necessity, assuming the free will of the parents, provided, however, that there is no law in that place that makes the contract of such children null and void.[6]

The first part of this conclusion is clear from what was said in disputation 33, for in grave necessity parents are allowed to sell both themselves and their children who are under their authority. I have spoken of the grave need of the infidel: Since slavery under the legal authority of Christians is for their own spiritual good, it is charity to purchase their freedom so that they may have a chance to become Christians. But, if they were already Christians, the law of charity would require not only that they should remain free but often that they should be aided, as has already been said in that same the disputation.

The second part is that it is indeed wrong to force these people to sell their freedom when they offer a fair price for food, but it is right to prefer the one who offers his freedom when it is impossible to help both. This is proved, since it is clear evidence of a certain tyranny against charity unto a neighbor when a seller is not satisfied with the fair price for the food that his neighbor needs and in addition wrests his freedom from him. Yet, when he cannot help both, and since slavery is more useful to the seller than the food, and since it is better for his spiritual salvation, the one who offers his freedom as the price should be preferred.

The third part is that it is not allowed to buy children from infidels

6. To be *doli capax* is a legal term that refers to someone being capable of criminal responsibility. In Spain, these included males older than ten and half years. *Partida* 1.1.21.

unless they are not in great need, which is evident because, excepting such [need], the natural law denies parents this kind of authority, nor can the positive right grant it against the well-being of those children. However, as we said in disputation 33, wherever the Imperial Law is not in force, even mothers may sell their children provided the fathers do not refuse, which often happens in India, where they tend to sell their children when famine rages. (10) Debt alone is not a sufficient reason for a father to sell his child in order to free himself from debt, unless the father himself is about to be subjected to slavery for his debt, whether justly or unjustly and according to the custom of his country or when he is about to be afflicted with some other terrible disease. In that case, he may give his child into slavery to free himself from a just or unjust imminent danger.

The fourth part: If someone were to buy those children whose parents do not suffer from great need, he would be bound to restore their freedom along with that of all other slaves who were subjected to slavery in that place. It is clear that the father's contract would be null and void in that event, inasmuch as it exceeds the limits of paternal authority, since the children have not given up their own freedom of which they are the masters. The very fact that someone uses a free man as a slave obliges him to make restitution for the services and profits that he has obtained from that slave to the extent that he has become richer by him, when he has used him entirely in good faith, truly believing him to be a slave. If he used him entirely in bad faith, he must make restitution for the full amount, as we will discuss below.

The remaining conclusion is clear: When people are masters of their own freedom, they can freely sell it, in the case of greatest need and even without any need at all, even if they sinned by squandering it, as has been said in disputation 33. For this reason, when the laws of the place where the contract is made are not violated, the contract is valid. The same applies to the contract and the agreement of a child who is capable of criminal responsibility, and if the father also consents and as long as no greater authority is required according to the laws of that place, then the contract is valid.

(11) This whole conclusion is very often of importance in some parts of India. However, one must note that, when there is a rumor that many

are being offered for sale who are not the children of those who are
selling them but rather have been taken by theft or when there are cases
that give rise to specific suspicions and conjectures on account of which
this fear is justified, then those who are so offered must not be bought,
unless a thorough examination has been made beforehand and it is
morally evident to the buyer that he [the slave] has been sold justly. If
he is bought in any other way, the buyer is bound by all that was said
at the end of the second conclusion. It is the same if someone buys a
child from a father or mother when no famine and greatest need have
been proved. Now, in some places in India, the confessors are obliged
to examine the penitents on this point when someone appears whose
social status and the nature of his business lead to the assumption that
he has bought slaves from infidels.

(12) There is serious concern about the price at which such slaves
are bought, including those who are imported from Guinea, especially
Lower Guinea. In some parts of India, they are bought out of their parent's hand, sometimes for the price of four or six royal silver [coins].
Similarly, in Guinea [they can be bought] for one of those mirrors that
the poor women among us use or for a few other goods or for a half cu-
bit of blue, green, or red cloth, [or] other goods of glass or brass, which
we do not value highly, and other similar things that among us are considered [of little value], so that sometimes to a merchant the price of a
slave would be no more than one gold coin or even less. The merchants
do not deny that this is so, and the tribute that they pay to the king, as
has been recalled above, is a testimony to this. It is also because the merchants themselves profit greatly from this business, as well as those others who are called *pombeiros* or *tangosmãos*, who mostly purchase the
slaves directly from the Africans and sell them back to the merchants.
Moreover, [they buy the slaves at low prices because] they have expenses
to feed the slaves while they are transported and sold in that kingdom,
and many of them perish before they are either sold or reach this kingdom, all of which could not happen if they had not been sold in Africa
for a very low price. Furthermore, since these places are extremely hot,
troublesome, and not at all conducive to health, no merchant would
want to go there unless he had the hope of making an enormous profit.

I would not dare to condemn this business in Guinea from this point of view, nor have I yet read of anyone who would condemn it or question it from this point of view. The reason is that these things, although they are considered of little value among us, are considered of the greatest value among them because of their poverty and because of the scarcity [of these goods], even though their rough and wild nature contributes to this.[7] Moreover, the transportation of these things over such a long distance by sea, with so much trouble and danger, greatly increases their price in those places, considering that the Africans are delighted with these things and consequently want to buy them. Likewise, the abundance of slaves, who are offered for sale in these places, makes their price much cheaper than if they were sold in smaller numbers. Also, the expense of taking the trouble of exporting slaves and the danger of transporting them and the fact that the slaves themselves or even the merchants may perish, justifiably makes their price much cheaper to the merchants than it would be if all these things did not intervene. In this matter, it is not the value of a human being as a human being or to the extent that he has been redeemed by the blood of Christ that is to be considered, as has been done by someone who has wondered whether this business is [morally] suspect for that reason alone, but rather the profit that the merchant makes by transporting the slave.

For this reason, as long as the exchange is in accordance with the value or estimate of the slaves as well as the merchandise [for which they are exchanged] in that place, I do not think that this business should be condemned from this point of view, at least if there is no further information about this business, especially considering that it [the business] was introduced such a long time ago, during which time no one has raised any concerns, and no other urgent reason presents itself to the contrary. All this is granted. The Africans themselves sell slaves to one another for the cheapest things in that region, which they nevertheless value, such as elephant skins, which are hung around their necks as ornament, for panther teeth, which are also hung around their the necks, and other similar things.

As for the other things that are sold in India at this low price, it would not be surprising if the reason [for the low price] were the price

7. On Molina's theory of just price, see *DIEI*, II.348.3.

for the food brought by the merchant and that he exchanges for the slave that, although the cost to the merchant is only four or six royal silver coins in the place from which the food is imported, is increased by the long sea voyage by which it is transported to alleviate the misery in the regions where the slaves are bought and by the scarcity in the place where the slaves are sold. Yet I hear that such slaves are sold in exchange for these very silver coins of the modest value mentioned.[8]

To the extent that we, being so far away from those places, can say anything about them according to what has reached our ears, it must be known that in the Kingdom of Cambay,[9] as in other kingdoms, where these slaves are bought, children used to be sold by their parents when famine was not very severe—so that there were not many who would sell their children under the compulsion of necessity—for six, eight, or ten pardaos, as they are called (this coin is worth a quarter of the value of the gold coin called a cruzado in Portuguese and a ducado in Spanish).[10] Now, children of this kind were taken to those places in India that fall under the jurisdiction of the king of Portugal, and they used to be sold to other Portuguese people for fifteen, twenty, twenty-five, thirty, forty, and sometimes fifty of the coins that are called pardaos, [depending on] the condition of the children. But when there is a severe famine in the Kingdom of Cambay, there are many who, under the pressure of necessity, sell their children and usually at a lower price so that neither they nor their children may perish; in that case they sell them at a very low price not only to the Portuguese but also to Muslims and other infidels to the spiritual detriment of the children.

8. The point is that it would be morally acceptable to buy slaves in India for an amount of food that costs only four or six reais in Portugal but costs more in India. However, this is not the case. Rather, the slaves are bought in India for four or six reais (or for the amount of food that can be bought for four or six reais at Indian prices, which is less than the amount of food that can be bought in Portugal with the same money). In other words, the Portuguese merchants buy children in India for unjustifiably low prices.

9. The Kingdom of Khambhat in Gujarat, India.

10. This was a coin specific to Portuguese India, deriving its name from a local coin called pratápa in Hindi and partab in Arabic. See Josephus Gerson da Cunha, *Contributions to the Study of Indo-Portuguese Numismatics* (Bombay: Education Society's Press: 1883), 47.

Now that these things have been established, I say, first, that if the common price for the children is not very low but rather high, there is no particular reason why one child should be bought for a lower price than others (for example, if his life is in great danger or if great expenses would be incurred in his care and feeding, [assuming] that he would die if left under the authority of his parents, etc.). If this child were to be bought at such a low price, the purchase would be unjust and the buyer would be bound by conscience to grant the child his freedom. He could not demand more work or time from it than for the amount of money for which [the child] was bought. Neither the ignorance of the seller nor his need excuse the buyer from the sin of having bought the child so cheaply, and he would be bound to restore his freedom in the way I have explained, since common necessity and the abundance of sellers did not cause this to be the customary price for children at that time [and] in that region. In fact, I say that, when it is not otherwise clear that one of the sellers is a parent of the child, it must be assumed from such a cheap price that the child has been stolen. But if such a presumption existed at the time of the purchase, so that the buyer could not have been a possessor in good faith from the beginning, the buyer would not only be obligated to conduct due moral diligence to know whether the child was stolen, but also, if nothing certain could be discovered about either possibility [whether he was stolen or not] then the [time] the child was forced to serve for the price [paid] must be reduced, in proportion to the amount of doubt about whether the child had been stolen, during which [time] the child was bound to serve for the price [paid].

I would then add the following: If, in view of the general need of men [to enslave children] and the great number of those who offered their own children for sale, this is indeed the common price for children at that time in that region, then I would not dare to apply the severity of justice to force the buyers to grant freedom to all the children who had been bought so cheaply and would rather be satisfied if they served only for a time that is more or less in proportion to the price. Neverthe-less, out of love for one's neighbor (which Christians especially owe to their fellow Christians) [and] assuming that the children have received baptismal water, they may not be possessed as perpetual slaves—nor sold to others as slaves—[but instead may be possessed only] for a certain amount of time or only for as long as those who buy them live and they may [only] use them as domestic servants [*famuli*] in proportion to the price paid, and if all the other attendant circumstances apply. Indeed, I hear that religious and God-fearing men in India advise and even command this, when they discover such things in confession or outside confession. The first part is proved by the fact that this price would be common and just for that merchandise in that region when the attendant circumstances apply. But the second part needs no further proof. Nevertheless, after ownership has been obtained for that cheap a price, strictly according to the standards of justice, I would not dare to impose this order and refuse to absolve him or to instruct him to make restitution to someone who has sold the child thus taken at a far higher price, but I would only advise him to make an arrangement with the slave's owner, if it is convenient for him to do so, by accepting a part of the price and releasing the slave after a certain time.

(13) Before we present the fourth conclusion, there are two doubts that certainly need to be examined. The first doubt arises when, after due moral diligence has been conducted (if such is possible), it is not clear to outsiders which of the two republics that are at war with each other is waging a just war but instead the matter is so ambiguous that outsiders may assume that both are waging a just war, not materially—since this cannot happen—but at least formally.[11] This may be assumed [that is, that the war can ostensibly be just on both sides] because, assuming that the republics in question are Christian,[12] it must be assumed that both sides have carefully weighed the reasons for war and that each is waging war based on the advice of learned men and, since moral matters can be doubtful on many occasions, there is room for many plausible opinions to be given in support of either side. I ask whether, in this case, it would be right for these outsiders to buy from one of these republics, either movable things captured by soldiers during the war or even prisoners. Furthermore, let us concede for the sake of argument that Christians could be reduced to slavery if captured by Christians. In the absence of a better judgment, I must

11. See note 6 in disputation 37.

12. Molina uses the term *res publica*, which is sometimes translated as "state." We wish to maintain the original meaning, so we translate it as "republic."

answer this doubt by saying that they could be lawfully bought and retained, so long as the buyer is willing, should the injustice of the war of that republic from which he buys them come to light, to give such slaves their freedom and to pay for the services and benefits that he had obtained from them, to whatever extent he had been enriched by them, and when the seller had not fully satisfied by those slaves [that is, if the requirements of justice had not been met]. Similarly, he must be prepared to return the other things bought or, if they no longer exist, the amount by which he was in any way enriched by them. Beyond that, [they can be kept] as long as he intends to zealously pursue an investigation when he has the opportunity or the hope of knowing whether the war waged by that republic was unjust after all.

(14) Covarrubias in *Regula peccatum, parte* 2, ss. 11, n. 6, thinks that by Imperial Law every republic at war in this way obtains ownership of the things captured by its soldiers during the war.[13] For this reason, it has been established by Imperial Law that, if our soldiers, even during the war, are fighting for the same cause [that is, the cause that justified launching the war] and take movable things from the enemies, for example, captured soldiers, they are not obliged to return them to the previous owners from whom the enemies took them. However, certain things are an exception for which the Imperial Law has granted the privilege of *postliminium*, [which states that] as soon as these things return to our borders, they return to the state they were in before they came into the hands of the enemy, so that their ownership returns to those to whom they belonged before.[14] Covarrubias says, for instance, that just as when a thief takes a thing by theft, he does not obtain ownership of it, nor does the previous owner lose his ownership, and for this reason this very thing acquired [by a third party] with whatever title must be returned to its previous owner, the same is the case when

13. Diego Covarrubias y Leyva, *Regulae peccatum. De regulis iuris libro VI Relectio* (Venice: Rubinus, 1569), pars II, sec. XI, n. 8 at 204.

14. The *ius posliminii*, which goes back to Roman Law, states that after captivity and return to the place of origin, the person formerly held captive has his rights restored; see Johann-Christoph Woltag, "Postliminium," in *Max Planck Encyclopedia of International Law* (https://opil.ouplaw.com/display/10.1093/law:epil/9780199231690/law-9780199231690-e378).

the injustice of the war waged by a republic is patent. Its soldiers do not obtain ownership of what they seize from the enemy republic; instead the ownership remains with those to whom the goods belonged, and so, if they were to be recovered in war [by a third party], they would not come to belong to those who recovered them, but they would have to be returned to the previous owners. If, however, it is thought that one of the two republics is waging a just war, [this law] does not apply, because what is captured in a war always becomes the property of the captor. By this reasoning, he says, the Romans prudently judged that, just as they intended to wage only just wars, equally the enemy might believe their war to be just, [and] establishing the law according to which [goods] captured in a war would come to belong to the captors, excepting some goods to which, for just reasons, they granted the privilege of *postliminium*. But, as we will see, many of the imperial regulations to which we refer on the subject of war openly show that the Imperial Law actually confirms our opinion [and not that of Covarrubias]. Because, since a war cannot materially and truly be just on both sides, then it cannot happen that the ownership of the things captured in a war can be obtained by both sides but only by those who have justice [on their side], even though [the other republic] might, in the grip of invincible ignorance, believe that [the enemy] is waging an unjust war. There would be no reason that would allow them to acquire ownership of the thing itself but only under the assumption and estimation of those who completely ignore that the republic is waging such an [unjust] war. Therefore, it is completely illicit to wage a war while believing in good conscience that the enemy will acquire ownership of the things captured in that war and that they can seize people who belong to this republic. For this reason, I do not think that these laws have any force in the court of conscience, nor, indeed, among Christians, in the court of law, as we shall discuss on the matter of war.[15] This means that these laws [cited by Covarrubias] are, in my judgment, ineffective to refute our opinion, but this must be explained elsewhere.

The reason that convinces me is this: because each of these republics, whether they are materially waging a just war at the same time or not,

---

15. Molina's theory of war is contained in disputations 98–123 of *De iustitia et iure*.

as long as they believe that the war is just on their part, can legitimately retain the goods thus captured and possess them as their own. The subjects of both republics, while princes are waging this war, even if they [the subjects] have doubts about whether the justice of the war is merited, nevertheless, as long as there is no injustice that is obvious to them, not only do they fight legitimately, but also, having been commanded by the prince, have an obligation to fight, and so they legitimately keep whatever they take in such a war, as we will show on the matter of war. Therefore, as long as they legitimately possess such things as their own, anyone could legitimately acquire this right [of ownership] and possess the things as their own with the same burden, that is, as soon as the injustice becomes apparent, they must restore them in the same way as they came to possess them. This is confirmed: Not only does [this rule] not cause any harm, but it actually brings considerable benefit to the people of the warring republics, because it increases the number of people who, when they realize the injustice of war, are individually forced to fully restore those things to their owners, when there is hope and opportunity to establish the injustice of war.

(15) Here is the second doubt: When it is clear to outsiders that two republics are waging a war iniquitously in the sense that they do not care whether the war is just or unjust and instead each of them, whether by justice or by injustice, seeks to rob and subjugate the other to itself. For this reason they refuse to come to terms with their enemies and instead want to continue the war and inflict mutual aggression on each other, as I am afraid are many of the wars among the infidels, especially among barbarians. I ask whether the goods captured from both sides [in these wars] would belong to the captors and whether, if people from both sides were captured in this war, they would become slaves of the captors and whether they could be bought by outsiders in good conscience as perpetual slaves.

To this doubt—barring a better judgment—I think it must be said, although it may seem harsh to admit, that in such an unjust war the captured things belong to those who capture them, at least when it is clear about both republics [i.e., that they fight without regard for justice], it is not improbable that they belong to those who capture them and that outsiders can buy them. At least after the purchase, I would not dare to order the buyers to restore these things, just as I would not advise such a transaction before the purchase. I am inclined to think that this is probable. First, even though these republics would commit a mortal sin by fighting in this war and even though they would be violating the fifth commandment of the Decalogue every time they killed someone, it would be wrong for any outsider to help one side. Nevertheless, there is in place a perverse contract or a quasi-contract in which by tacit or explicit mutual consent they wanted the things captured by each side to belong to the captors, so that the republic that prevails subjugates the other [republic].[16] This is no different from a perverse contract by which someone agrees with a woman on a price to gain access to her body in violation of the sixth commandment of the Decalogue or in which someone makes an agreement with someone else to kill a third person unjustly, [a contract which] is nevertheless equal for both sides. Just as in the case there is an agreement to fornicate or to kill another person unjustly, those who make the agreement are bound to withdraw completely from the contract, and yet, if either the woman gives access to herself or one person kills the other unjustly, by justice [the first party] owes them the money that becomes theirs when it comes into their possession; here this is also the case. In the same way, those [republics] who wage war unjustly are always bound to withdraw from the war and yet what they seize they make their own out of that perverse, and at the same time fair, tacit or explicit contract. In fact, if one of the republics at war without just cause were to almost defeat the other, the defeated republic should sue for peace, although the victorious republic would be bound to refrain from the war in the sense that it could not justly kill anyone; it could, however, justly capture and subject its opponents. For, under similar circumstances, the enemy would have done the same for his own republic, and, having done so, by the power of that implied and equal contract, whatever was taken is rightfully his. As I have already said, I am led to think this not only because the condition of the two republics is equal but also because—since damage and injustice are inflicted and have been done to both sides and since neither party is

16. According to *Institutes* 3, 27, a quasi-contract is an obligation "as though from a contract," that is, without a written contract.

willing to make restitution to the other for the damages done—clearly each person by the tacit or explicit consent of his own republic may retain what he has taken from the enemy in that war as compensation for the damages that they have inflicted on his republic and that they are willing to inflict. Moreover, it would be difficult to order each of these warring republics to return to its enemies what it has taken from them and [to compensate] for the damages it caused if the enemy republic was unwilling or unready to return what it had taken and [to compensate for] the damages it had caused. But, if such people could legally keep what they had taken in such an unjust war, it is clear that any outsider could legally acquire from them the right they have thus obtained over things and to possess them in a similar manner. Based on this chapter, there will certainly be no shortage of people who will want to ease the consciences of those who purchase slaves from the infidels in either Guinea or Cafreria and who import them into this kingdom and other places and who will dare to promote this business as just and lawful.

(16) Nevertheless, let there be a fourth conclusion: It seems to me much more likely that the business of buying slaves in this way from the infidels in these places and importing them from there is unjust and unfair and that all those who practice it sin mortally and that they are in a state of eternal damnation unless they can be excused by invincible ignorance, which I dare say none of them are in. In the meantime, [I think] the king and all those who hold the keys to the kingdom in their hands, especially the bishops of Cape Verde and the island of São Tomé, and those who hear the confessions of all of them, each according to their rank and order, must take care to examine these matters and to decide what should be permitted and what should not. They should see to it that injustices are effectively curtailed in the future, unless they know something about these things that I do not or unless there are other principles that shed light on them that I do not know. I am led to think the following: it is a mortal sin, not only against charity but also against justice with the burden of restitution, to buy things of which there is a probable or just suspicion (although if one is blinded by greed, one may not care about that) that they were bought with an unjust title and that they do not belong to the sellers. Anyone who buys things in order to keep them entirely for himself and about which he ought to presume

that they have probably been obtained by theft, clearly sins mortally, if [he does so] without prior examination by which it would be known for certain that they have not been obtained by theft, and if he is not a possessor in good faith from the outset, he is obliged afterward to conduct due diligence to find out whether the thing he has bought belonged to another person. If he finds this out, he is bound to restore it completely, but if he is unable to find out anything with certainty, he is bound to restore part of the value in proportion to the remaining amount of doubt as to whether it belongs to another person, which may be more or less, depending on the amount of doubt. Therefore, from what has been said on this matter here and in the preceding disputation and from what we will now expound, whoever buys slaves from infidels in these places should rightly convince himself that most of them have been reduced to slavery without a just title. By buying them without inquiring into the title under which they were subjected to slavery and without a just cause for rejecting the presumption that suggests or could suggest the contrary, he effectively sins mortally. He would not possess them in good faith, but he would be bound to inquire about the truth as soon as the opportunity arises. But if it [the opportunity] does not present itself—and it does not commonly present itself—he would be bound to make restitution to the slave (to the detriment of whose freedom the purchase was made) in proportion to the amount of doubt or of the suspicion that remains: not of a part of the slave's value but according to the [strength] of the interest that the slave would have had in being free, which is clearly greater than the benefit that others derive from this slavery and therefore also greater than the value [of the slave] compared with that of other slaves. I said: "But according to the [strength] of the interest that the slave would have had in being free" because that is the damage that he has inflicted on the slave, which must be restored to him and not merely the value of his services.

It only remains for us to prove the minor [premise] of this whole argument.[17] Surely, those who buy slaves from the hands of infidels in those places should convince themselves that they have mostly been

17. Scholastic arguments often use the basic notions of Aristotelian syllogistics, dividing them into a major and a minor premise in order to reach a conclusion. In the conclusion, the major term is the predicate and the minor term is the subject.

reduced to slavery with an unjust title, which outweighs other [consid-
erations]. In order to arrive at a higher principle, I submit first this. It is
the common conclusion of the jurists, as we have shown in the matter
of war, that it is wrong for outsiders to help in battle one of the two
republics at war with each other as long as there is doubt as to which of
them has a just cause for war against the other. And it is wrong for [out-
siders to help] for the same reason, [that is], without any further inquiry into the justice of the war, to help either of them due to the danger
that, if one republic were to uphold justice, it would be treated unjustly
if it were fought against in this way. Therefore, the jurists rightly affirm
that, whenever outsiders fight in this way without prior inquiry, they
sin mortally, not only against charity but also against justice. They are
not considered to be possessors in good faith of what they seize in the
war but they are obliged to inquire afterward about the injustice of the
war, and, when this has been established, they are bound to make full
restitution for what they have seized in this way and, in addition, for all
the damage they have caused. But, if the warring parties cannot be sure
of the justice or injustice of the war, they are bound to make restitution
for a part of the damage and the things they have taken in proportion to
the amount of doubt, even if nothing is left over, and even if they have
not become richer by these things. This is because of the sin of injustice
that they have committed by fighting in this way.

Having established this, I say [this]: Just as these people, for this
reason, sin mortally against justice and because they are not considered
to be possessors in good faith of what they have taken in such a war,
they are obliged to make restitution in the way we have explained. So
also outsiders who, without any inquiry into the justice of the war, buy
without distinction slaves captured in a war from one of the warring
republics—and especially slaves who have been reduced to slavery by
a title of such a war—sin mortally against justice because of the danger
to which they expose themselves by buying slaves who do not belong
to the sellers.[18] By buying them, they do the gravest injustice to the
slaves [themselves], that is, they buy their slavery, or rather their free-

18. The implication of this is clear. The Portuguese, as outsiders of conflicts between African tribes, cannot licitly acquire slaves from either side, and so they are
severely at fault.

dom, which the captives have not lost and over which they [still] retain ownership. As has been explained, they are also bound to restore this freedom to these very slaves. This alone would be enough to condemn the slave trade that we are discussing as the mortal sin of injustice, since the Portuguese would not ask the Africans about the justice of their war, nor about the other titles by which the slaves they sell are reduced to slavery, but would buy without any distinction [the slaves] that are brought to them.

(17) Let us now turn our attention to the wars among Africans. Clearly it must be assumed that they are very rarely just. Indeed, there are those among them who consider themselves more powerful and who unjustly invade others and try to oppress them. However, these are the ones who bring back the greater booty of saleable slaves, while others suffer injustice by unjustly losing their freedom, becoming slaves. A trustworthy person who lived among the Cafres for a long time and who had hardly any scruples about buying slaves in this way, told me that in this region there was one king among other [kings] who had bold and unusually fierce subjects, whom the rest of the people feared greatly. This king, in order to gather a large number of slaves for profit, used to attack the neighboring areas at night, with soldiers distributed in different villages so that some could attack one village and others another at the same time. Yet, as soon as they reached the neighboring regions, upon their arrival they would begin to shout and proclaim at the top of their lungs, admonishing [the locals] to look after their best interest and to realize that they [the invaders] had superior and more powerful weapons and, unless they gave up a certain number [of inhabitants] for slavery, they would all be killed. These miserable people, terrified that they would all be slaughtered, would then go into a house and take from it a son or a daughter and close the door, and another would take one of the wives, etc. In this way the captives were taken away and sold. One companion of our father Gonçalo da Silveira referred to this custom of these people, among others, and wrote to us that their barbarity was so great that someone who had been robbed would steal from another person, using as a justification that he had been robbed by others before.[19] From this it is clear how seldom it can

___

19. Gonçalo da Silveira (1526–61).

be supposed that the wars between the Africans are just so that merchants may buy from them slaves who have been reduced to slavery by a title of war, without any further inquiry and with a safe conscience.

According to what has been said in the second doubt of the fourth conclusion, much less can it be believed that the wars among the Africans arise from a quasi-common agreement and a tacit pact and that the different republics wickedly want to wage war against each other. Therefore, in this slippery and jagged matter, the merchants can never claim that they are justly buying slaves that have been obtained on account of a title of war. Even if there were a probable conjecture that sometimes the wars among the Africans were of this kind and if we were to grant that the merchants had the right to buy slaves obtained in such a war, they could not buy them lawfully and justly until it was clear to them that the [slaves] bought in a particular case would be reduced to slavery in such a war or any other just war.[20] In fact, if they were to buy them without any inquiry, or if they were in doubt as to whether they had been justly reduced to slavery, they would sin mortally against charity and justice and they would be bound to make restitution in the way that I have explained above.

(18) As to the wars of the Africans, by which they usually seize the slaves sold by the Portuguese (according to what the merchants themselves answer when they are asked, without being compelled by threats of torture), I think that it is not a war but theft. In order to have [slaves] ready [for sale], while the ships of the Portuguese are mooring there, or even before they moor, those who live in certain villages under [the command of] a lord come by night or at other times to attack neighboring places to plunder and take with them slaves by force, but they rarely form armies and meet in battle. They have no fortresses and their villages have no defense other than palisades and trees. So, the Portuguese trade seems to be an opportunity and incitement for them to engage in plundering these people. It [the plundering] is certainly much more frequent and involves a greater number of people than if this trade did not exist. This is especially true in the Guineas, which

20. Even if the reasons for a just war were just, the merchants could only acquire slaves obtained in such a war if they had previously done their due diligence, thus knowing for certain that it was a just war.

the Muslim merchants do not have access to nor do we know of any others who engage in this kind of business other than our people [the Portuguese], all of which corrupts and condemns the business.

And what shall we say, if we add to this that the slaves sometimes imported to be sold are not captured from foreign villages but are taken by theft from the towns of the very same captors, and, besides, how many other slaves were sold by the Portuguese in these places without a crime sufficient for the punishment of perpetual slavery and without just cause for them to be subjected to sale into slavery by their own parents, spouses, and lords of their own villages? From what has been said in the second conclusion and in the preceding disputation, it is clear that many are sold in this way and, when this is connected with the third conclusion, then you will find, from the confession of the merchants themselves, that the minor [premise] of this proposition is sufficiently proved, on the proof of which so much has been said. At the same time, you will also find that the fourth conclusion has also been proven.

Here I do not want to say anything about the savagery with which these slaves are sometimes treated when they are transported from the interior regions to the ships by those who are called *tangosmãos* or *pombeiros*. It is reported that sometimes someone's arm is cut off and that he is left to die and that others are beaten with it [the arm] as if it were a whip and they are forced to make this journey, out of fear of dying, [but there are] other savageries inflicted on them. While these wretched people are being torn from their own people, being conquered, and being led away in this way, they delay their abduction and refuse to go on, partly out of love for their land, partly out of fear of slavery or the horror of death (indeed, they fear that they will be killed and devoured). In fact, those who lead them are sometimes not satisfied with any pace they take. Nor will I say anything about the savagery that is often committed on the voyages when they are being transported, nor [will I say anything] about the numerous [merchants] who, in order to make more profit, export so many that a large number of them will necessarily die because of the narrowness of the ship in which they are confined night and day as if in prison. I will not say anything about the concubinage that many of the *tangosmãos* or the merchants have with the women they export and whom they take for their own service in places where they do not have wives. I will not say anything about the concubinage of the slaves themselves, when men and women are transported together. These and similar vices of those engaged in this business do not make the business itself unjust or essentially illicit but should be treated with caution in what concerns the governors of these provinces and of this kingdom and [in what concerns] other ministers of the king. Perhaps it would be useful to enact some laws on this matter. All these things taken together may be a reason why very few merchants, if any, become rich by entering into such a business. As I have heard from the merchants themselves, God does not look favorably upon them because of the many sins they commit. If only there were no graver misfortunes, as many fear, because of the nature of this business that has been ignored for so long!

(19) Nevertheless, let there be a fifth conclusion: As long as there are neither preachers nor other ministers of the Church among all these nations (in which a great door [to salvation] has evidently been opened and that may close because of our inactivity) who care for what belongs to Jesus Christ, we should, for this reason, support the slavery under pious men, as far as it can be done with a good conscience, because those wretched captives receive such a great good as faith and thus abandon that barbarous and impious cesspool of humanity so that they may live and end their lives among Christians, even if it [the Christian life] is associated with the misery of perpetual slavery. But, since evil must not be done for the sake of a good and since those who export these people do not seek a spiritual good but rather their own temporal gain, this business should not be allowed to continue beyond this, nor should the confessors of the Episcopate of Cape Verde, nor those on the island of São Tomé, nor those who hold the key to this kingdom allow more than what justice and the love for one's neighbor permit. I will also say that I am uncertain by what right the kings of Portugal can forbid other Christian nations from having commerce with these infidels as the Portuguese do unless they are assisted by preachers and ministers of the Gospel. This should be so, for this is the reason why this kind of commerce has been granted by the popes only to them [the Portuguese], and this is the only sufficient reason to forbid other nations (although it is otherwise common by the law of nations) [to trade slaves]. But,

if capable ministers of the Gospel should be sent to those barbarous nations and if in their regions they were to be converted to the faith, then clearly all the pious [men] should rather consider and favor the freedom of these wretched people. And their slavery should only be permitted when it is clearer than light that it is just, either because the cause of freedom is indeed the most pious and it should be supported as such or because it would be of great help in propagating our Christian faith and customs in those places. If these godly things were taken care of and if we were satisfied to have another just way of trading with these nations, then God, who generously rewards good works, would give easy access to the many gold and silver mines in these places and he would make agriculture profitable, for example, on the island of São Tomé. There would be manifold benefits and profits from other things done by slaves and at the same time it would protect all our interests. One should be satisfied if there were no other profit than to have one's conscience saved from eternal condemnation.

It has often been emphasized that these merchants, to the extent that they either buy slaves directly from the Africans or import them from there, are bound to make restitution when it is not clear with moral certainty that the slave bought was reduced to slavery by a just title. (20) There are two things I would like to point out. The first is that there is a considerable difference between someone who, believing that something seems to be his own but not being completely certain, secretly takes it from someone who has begun to possess it in good faith and someone who, doubting whether the thing being sold or given to him is stolen, receives it, either for a price or for free. The first is completely obligated to make restitution in full, because he has seized it in this way. But the second is only bound to make a partial restitution in [proportion to] the amount of doubt as to whether it has belonged to another [person].

The reason for this distinction is that, although it is not certain that what a person has begun to possess in good faith is not his own, there is no law that requires him to deprive himself of that thing in whole or in part, even when he has rightly begun to doubt whether the thing belongs to him. He is not obliged to return any part of it, even if he is absolutely convinced that the thing does not belong to him in any way, because in case of doubt the condition of the possessor is better when the possession began in good faith.[21] But, if the thing is received from someone on the basis of a free title or with a payment and if the person who accepts it has doubts about whether the thing belongs to another person, he may accept it considering that [the other person] had rights, either certain or doubtful, over the entirety of what he hands over. Therefore, it happens that he is bound to carefully examine whether it belongs to another [person other than the seller] and, if he finds that it does belong to another, he would be bound to fully return it. However, if there is doubt as to whether it belongs to the one who gave it to him or to another, he would be bound to restore it only in proportion to the amount of doubt because, although he himself has never begun to possess it in good faith, he does not know that the thing belongs to someone else and that someone has been unjustly deprived of his own possession. For these reasons, we say that the buyer of something about which there is doubt as to whether it belonged to the seller at the time of sale is not bound to make full restitution until it is not absolutely clear that it did not belong to the seller.

(21) Second: If it should happen under some circumstances that someone has bought slaves from the aforesaid merchants in invincible ignorance of the fact that they were not reduced to slavery by a just title, even after this ignorance had been dispelled, and after he had reason to doubt whether they were reduced to slavery by a just title, he would indeed be bound to conduct due moral diligence, so as to find out whether they had been reduced to slavery unjustly. In the meantime, however, as long as this is unclear, he would not be bound to make any restitution at all since, in case of doubt, the condition of the

---

21. The point is that a possessor cannot be forcibly deprived of his possessions simply because he no longer possesses them in good faith. On the notion of the principle of *conditio possidentis*, Rudolph Schüßler notes, "The Possessor Principle in its traditional interpretation implies that those who want to deprive a possessor of her possession incur the burden of proof of unlawful possession." *The Debate on Probable Opinions in the Scholastic Tradition* (Leiden and Boston: Brill, 2019), 95. Regarding the problem of enslavement, Molina understands this principle to refer to the possession that all people have over their own freedom, which means that the one who intends to deprive a person of his or her freedom must prove that it is legally and morally legitimate to do so.

one who initially began his possession in good faith is better. If, on the other hand, he finds that they had been reduced to slavery unjustly, he would be bound to restore freedom to the slaves, if they are still alive, and [to restore the amount] by which he has become richer through their service or in some other way, of which we shall give a fuller account in the following disputation concerning similar circumstances.

Disputation 36

Whether those who possess slaves in this kingdom
or any other, which we have talked about in the
fourth conclusion of the preceding disputation,
can licitly retain them and can licitly buy them

Summary

1. Those who purchase slaves from a merchant in good faith can licitly retain them. What are they obliged to do if they start to have doubts regarding the title or if they reach certainty as to their injustice?

2. What a possessor in good faith is obliged to do when he establishes that the slave has been subjected unjustly.

3. To what extent someone who is convinced that the slaves have been unjustly subjected [to slavery] can retain them when they were not bought from a merchant but purchased in good faith from a third party.

4. When someone buys [slaves] in good faith from a merchant who brings them from Africa without having reason to doubt its justice.

5. The obligations of those who have doubts regarding the just enslavement of a slave bought from a merchant who exports him or from a third party who did not possess him in good faith at first.

We have already talked of the foul well the slaves who are brought from Guinea and Cafreria come from. Now we must talk about the streams that stem from it in order to calm the conscience of men. For this reason, in this disputation the account will not be about the merchants who bring them from those places but about the other possessors who acquire them from them [these merchants].

(1) First conclusion: Whoever has bought such slaves in good faith from merchants or from someone who possesses them after obtaining them from others who at some point in time started to possess them in good faith can licitly retain them, as happens with all the kinds of possessors we are talking about in this disputation. Assuming that doubt arises because of what has been said in the preceding disputations or if there are other reasons to doubt whether they have been reduced to slavery justly, they [the slaves] are retained licitly without an obligation to restore [their freedom] until they [the buyers] come to convince themselves that the particular [slaves] they possess were not subjected to slavery by means of a just title, which, however, rarely occurs.[1] If there is, however, a way that gives hope of acquiring certainty about whether they were not subjected to slavery by means of a sufficient title, do [buyers] have an obligation to make inquiries? If they omitted this or if the omission was the reason for not knowing the truth later or for not knowing it well enough, they are bound to restore to the slave, by the appraisal of a prudent man, a greater or lesser [value] according to how much it would have been in the slave's interest [of finding out the truth]. If afterward it is somehow shown with certainty that the slave has been justly reduced to slavery, then the obligation to restore [the value] ceases since it is in itself obvious that the culpable omission to conduct an inquiry regarding the titles did no harm [to the slave]. When the slave establishes that he has been unjustly reduced to slavery, even if he gives an account of the unjust way he was reduced to slavery, it is usually not enough for the possessor to be convinced of that matter, because he could rightly be afraid that he [the slave] might lie and pretend because of his desire to be free. If someone, however, was convinced of the matter without any doubt, he would be obliged to give him his freedom and do everything that we shall discuss in the following conclusion.

First and foremost, what we intend to establish in this lengthy conclusion arises from what is manifest: That all [merchants] are either

---

1. This has been established in the previous disputation.

possessors in good faith of their slaves from the beginning or they succeeded to the right over slaves while, at some point in time, a possessor
in good faith existed. As has been shown at the end of the preceding
conclusion, whoever starts to possess [something] in good faith is not
obliged to restore it until he acquires the certainty that the thing he
possesses is not his, because in case of doubt, the condition of the possessor is better.

Moreover, the subjects do not have the obligation to examine
whether the goods that are brought to this kingdom and sold in it are
lawfully taken away and sold by the subjects of this kingdom. Rather,
[this obligation] belongs to the prince and his ministers and the subjects are to trust the foresight and administration of their superiors. So,
all those who have hitherto bought slaves, either from the merchants
themselves or from others, will be possessors in good faith and will
easily and deservedly be considered as such. Although that which we
have said in the preceding disputation seems to prove that many slaves
transported from those places have been unjustly subjected to slavery,
it nonetheless does not prove that of each and every slave nor of any
particular [slave].

What remains to be added to this conclusion does not require further proof, mostly because it is obvious that a possessor in good faith
cannot continue to possess it in good faith as soon as a doubt arises as
to whether the thing he possesses is his and that in his conscience he is
obliged to inquire about the true justice, so that he has to restore it if he
finds out that the thing he possesses is not his. If he were to omit this,
he would therefore be obliged to restore it to someone else according
to the extent of hope of finding out that it belonged [to the other per-
son] and also according to the extent of the likelihood of the damage
that this omission had inflicted on him. After having established that
there was a culpable omission, if it is shown that the thing has truly
belonged to someone else and this would have been found out if due
diligence had been conducted, then certainly the one who has omitted
[finding out] should not only restore [the thing to the owner] but also
the products and profits he received from it from the time of this omission. In the current discussion, however, he is obliged to restore to the
slave, apart from his freedom, the benefits and profits gained from the

time of the omission, even if they [the slaves] did not make him [the owner] wealthier.

(2) Second conclusion: When the possessor in good faith or the one who succeeds a possessor in good faith in rightfully [owning] a slave knows with certainty that the slave has been unjustly subjected to slavery, he is obliged to restore his freedom notwithstanding the price for which he was bought even if it is very high. [The possessor] should not be reimbursed for [that price] from the slave but rather from the seller.

Moreover, he is bound to compensate for services provided to him and any other benefit if he received any from him, however, only to the extent that he has become richer from these, which would happen on account of the failure of others who unjustly subjected him to servitude, who without a doubt are bound to restore everything to him more than anyone else because they are the principal and unjust cause of all damages done. If it was a handmaid and if her children or other descendants were captives due to the title of birth, the freedom of all of them would have to be restored and all the services and gains would have to be compensated if he [the possessor] received them from them inasmuch as he has gotten wealthier. If some of the aforementioned slaves are killed, then [the possessor] is obliged to restore to the heirs the received [value] of the services and gains that had made him wealthier. If [the slave] does not have an heir, then [the value] has to be restored to the poor or it has to be expended for another pious purpose in favor of the soul of the slave. This whole conclusion does not require proof, since a possessor in good faith is obliged to restore [the value] when he finds out that the thing is not his, even though he is not obliged to make restitution because of an unjust reception [of the thing], since it was not his fault. However, on account of the possession of the thing and of the benefits he received, which have made him wealthier, when he buys something that does not belong to him, he must make restitution for the amount by which he became wealthier [because of the slave's labor]. This happens when there is another person who, as the principal unjust cause of the damage, has the duty to make restitution but fails to do so. Nonetheless, it is the [buyer's] right to take legal action against the seller and to demand a [sum] that reflects his interest for the sale to be valid and for the thing purchased to have truly belonged to the seller.

(3) Third conclusion: Even after someone is persuaded by what has been established in the two preceding disputations—or by some other reason—that the slaves that were brought from the aforementioned places had mostly been reduced to slavery in an unjust fashion, he may licitly buy them, not while they are possessed by the merchant who exports them but after someone started to possess them in good faith. He would afterward be obliged to do moral due diligence in order to know whether the slave, either bought or received as a gift, has begun to be possessed in such a way that from the beginning he has been legitimately reduced to slavery, assuming that there was a way to know this for certain. If there was no such way, and normally there would be none, or if having done moral due diligence he did not find out with certainty [the origin of the slave], he is not obliged to restore anything to the slave and he can licitly possess him. The conclusion is proven because, as has been shown, the one who at some point in time possessed that slave and who received that title has a legitimate right over the slave. If doubt arises as to whether they were from the beginning legitimately reduced to slavery, then those [persons] are obliged to do moral due diligence if there is an appropriate way to establish with certainty the truth of the issue, yet they are not obliged to restore [anything] before learning with certainty that they [the slaves] were unjustly reduced to slavery. Therefore, others can buy or receive them for free when they are willing to assume their obligations. This certainly does not happen to the detriment and disadvantage of the slaves but rather it is good and convenient, since those other [people], having established that it is likely that those slaves have been unjustly subjected to slavery, will be more careful, their conscience being pricked, and it will motivate them to apply more intensely, as much as is humanly possible, due diligence to gain knowledge whenever there is hope to establish the truth. We must exempt from this conclusion the case of slaves who remain in the possession of their previous owners; here the truth of the matter could be established more easily and the slaves could more easily be given their freedom. Yet, after they have been transported to remote areas, they are deprived of such a benefit, which, however, rarely happens.

(4) Fourth conclusion: Whoever in the future buys those slaves in good faith from the hands of merchants who brought them from Africa,

because reasons for doubting whether they had been justly enslaved from the beginning did not reach their ears or because for any other reason they were their possessors in good faith, can retain them with a safe conscience until it is certain that they had been unjustly reduced to slavery. The conclusion is proven because they are truly possessors in good faith and their condition is better in the case of doubt, and, in that case, they can retain them [the slaves].

(5) The last conclusion: Whoever has doubts because of our arguments or for other reasons and [nonetheless] buys or receives such slaves from the hands of the merchants who transport them or [if they receive them] from any other person who has not initially possessed them in good faith or from a person who has not received a title [of property] of someone who possessed them in good faith is certainly obliged to make restitution to the slaves to the greater or lesser extent of the amount of doubt about whether they have initially justly been reduced to slavery. The conclusion is proven because neither he nor his predecessors are possessors in good faith such that the condition of the possessors themselves is better. Since they acquired [the slaves] with a doubtful right, that is, [doubting] whether the predecessors had justly possessed them, they are obliged to make restitution to the slaves according to a prudent judgment with respect to the amount of the doubt.

Disputation 37

Whether a slave legitimately reduced to slavery may flee to reunite with his people

Summary

1. Those unjustly captured may flee and their capturers and his associates have to make restitution for injustices and damages suffered.

2. Those who have sold themselves, [those who have been sold] by their parents, or [those] who have been born into slavery because they are children of a mother who has been reduced to slavery by any of these titles cannot licitly escape, nor can those who have been captured and condemned to slavery as a punishment for their crime.

3. Whether slaves reduced to this condition by the right of war and whether the child of a mother reduced to slavery by the right of war, may escape.

4. Covarrubias and Soto affirm this.

5. It is concluded that slaves captured in a just war have less value than do those reduced to slavery by other just titles.

6. Also, it is wrong to punish those slaves if they flee to join their own people, though it is permitted to restrain them so that they do not flee. See also number 10.

7. Also, these fugitive slaves may not use force against their pursuers.

8. Also, those who give advice or help these slaves to flee are not bound to make any restitution, unlike what happens with other slaves.

9. [Covarrubias and Soto's view] [r]ejected by the theory of others.

10. The person justly captured in a just war, when the justice of the capture and the injustice of his enemy is evident, sins mortally if he flees, and he must restore himself, even if he has returned to his people.

11. Someone who is justly condemned to a punishment and who is expected to execute and serve it himself has a duty of conscience to implement it.

12. This first conclusion is qualified.

13. What a person, captured in a war that is not so evidently just that the other part does not even formally wage it justly, can be obliged and forced to do.

14. The arguments for the affirmative answer are solved.

15. The prize of those who capture fugitive slaves and the punishment for concealing them.

(1) There is no doubt that these men, who have been detained as captives without just title, may flee to their people or to whom they wish. This is the case since in the war of the Turks and the Moors against us is unjust on their part, there is no doubt that our people, who have been detained there as captives, can licitly flee, if they wish, openly or secretly, and even by force, and anyone can licitly help them in their escape. Moreover, it is right for them to receive compensation for the injuries and damages they have received, as well as for the services they have given. Since our side is at perpetual war with them, they should not only receive adequate compensation for the damages and injustices from those who inflicted the injustice, because in those regions there is no one to impart justice but also to seize it from them as well as from others, according to the right of war and from the supposed will of our princes, whoever they be, as long as no particular case were to produce a public scandal. This is acknowledged by Cajetan in almost all cases according to the commentary on the *Secunda secundae* q. 66, a. 8.[1]

(2) This question therefore only applies to the case of captives who are subjected to slavery by a legitimate title. And among the jurists

---

1. Thomas de Vio (Cardinal Cajetan), *Commentaria in Summa Theologiae*, in Thomas Aquinas, *Opera omnia iussu impensaque Leonis XIII P. M. edita: Secunda secundae Summae theologiae; tomus nonus* (Rome: Typographia Polyglotta S.C. de Propaganda Fide, 1897), 94.

there is no controversy in this regard. They all agree that those who sold themselves or were legitimately sold by their parents or who were born to a mother already subject to slavery by one of these two titles cannot licitly flee, because, if they flee, they must restore themselves [to slavery] and pay the resulting damages to their owner, if there are any. Regarding captives who have been subjected to perpetual slavery as a punishment for their crimes, although the jurists did not say anything about them, I believe they would have said the same. Indeed, just as the person justly condemned to exile cannot flee but is obliged to execute or implement the punishment himself, so also those who have been subjected to slavery as a punishment will be obliged to inflict on themselves the punishment that was justly imposed on them by a sentence. Here the reason is the same. (3) There is only a controversy among the jurists about whether those slaves reduced to slavery under the law of war and of children born to a mother already reduced to slavery under the law of war can flee to their people.

(4) Covarrubias in I *Variarum resolutionum*, cap. 2, num. 10, and *Regulae peccatum* par. 2, §11, num. 6, asserts that they [the slaves] may flee, and, by the very fact that they cross the boundaries in which the captives are held, they obtain their freedom.[2] Because, he says, as long as they do not cross the boundaries, they do not obtain their freedom and therefore they should not flee in order to move within the boundaries [of the possessor's land], because they would harm their owner by depriving him of the service owed since the owner has not lost ownership over them. Concerning the gloss to the chapter *Ius gentium*, d. 1, under *Servitutes*, he responds that it must be understood that the captive of a just war sins if he flees from the authority of his owner without the intention of trespassing the boundary, because in this case he does not become free, but not when he flees to return to his people.[3] Soto, also, in book 4 of *De iustitia et iure*, question 2, article 2, [writes] that no one should bind slaves captured in a just war by placing them under so much [moral] distress that they cannot flee to their people.[4]

Covarrubias confirms his [Soto's] opinion using the law *Nihil in-*

2. Vio, *Commentaria in Summa Theologiae*, II-II, q. 66, a. 8.

3. Accursius, *Glossa in Digestum Vetus*, Dig. 5.1. at 5.

4. Domingo de Soto, *De la justicia y el derecho* (Madrid: Instituto de Estudios

terest, following *De captivis et postliminio reversis*, from which we can deduce his own opinion. He does so by referring to *Partida* VII, title 14, law 23, of the Castilian laws, where it is expressly established that, if a Saracen who has been justly captured by our people flees [and] then, by the sheer fact of reaching his people, he recovers his freedom, so that if he later freely returns with the intention of engaging in trade among us, he cannot be forced to return to slavery; and the same is deduced from law 23 of title 29 of *Partida* III.[5]

(5) From this opinion, some conclude first that the slave captured in a just war has a lower value than do slaves subjected under other just titles of slavery, because he can much more easily than others avoid being owned without any guilt and against the will of the owner. (6) Second, [they conclude that] it is not licit to punish those who flee to join their people, since a just punishment cannot be exacted unless there is guilt, but they do not do anything blameworthy by joining their people. (7) They add, however, that it is licit to shackle or chain those [slaves] so that they do not flee. They also add that, while it is licit for those slaves to escape and, while fleeing, to try not to fall into the hands of those who pursue them in the name of and under orders of their owners, it is not licit for them [the fugitive slaves] to inflict violence on them, in the same way that it would be licit for criminals to flee public servants who pursue them, but it is not licit for them [the fugitives] to use force against them. Otherwise a just war on both sides would ensue formally and materially.[6] (8) Third, those who provide the slave with advice and

<hr>

Políticos,1967), Spanish trans. by Marcelino Gonzáles Ordóñez, with fascimile of *De iustitia et iure*, Salamanca 1556 edition, lib. IV, q. 2, a. 2 at 290.

5. Cod. 8.50.10; *Siete partidas* (1555), vol. 2, partida 3, tit. 29, ley 23 at 170b.

6. Molina considers that a war that is just on both sides is impossible if preceded by a material injustice (*iniuria materialis*), that is, the factual violation of rights. This excludes the other side of being right, too. However, if it is preceded by a formal injustice (*iniuria formalis*), it can be construed as being just on both sides, in the sense that both sides could have, from their point of view, just reasons to engage in war, when they are truly convinced to have a just cause. In any case, a war cannot be materially and formally be just on both sides; see *DIEI*, II.103, col. 617a and col. 618b–c: "Quando vero utraque pars sibi persuaderet rem absque ullo omnino dubio ad se pertinere, alteramque partem non sine culpa non velle a lite desistere, saltem quia vel non quantum oportet … hac ratione potest saepe esse bellum iustum formaliter ex utraque parte."

help so that he may flee do not owe any restitution to the owner, since they cooperated in what is just and licit, but those who provide advice and help for other slaves to escape [that is, slaves not captured in just war] must restore to the owner the value of the slave and any resulting damages.

(9) A conflicting opinion clearly appears in the cited gloss, which generally states that a slave taken in a just war commits a sin if he escapes from his owner.[7] And to the law *Nihil interest*, which is cited as a counterexample, [the holder of this opinion] responds that [this law] must be understood [to apply] in the case that the war is unjust on the side of the captors. This opinion is embraced by Torquemada and many others that he [Covarrubias] cites, Antoninus in part 3, tit. 3, c. 6, n. 4, of his *Summa*, Fortunio in his commentary on the law *manumissiones, de iustitia et iure*, and Azpilcueta in his *Manual de confesores*, chapter 17, number 103, who treats this question to a greater extent in the latest edition.[8]

(10) Let this be our first conclusion: The one captured in a just war, when the justice of the captors and the injustice of the enemy is manifest, sins mortally if he flees his owner, and he must restore himself to him, even if he has joined his people. This is shown first, because the possessor was legitimately and undoubtedly his owner and, by escaping he stole himself from him, according to the law *De servis fugitivis*.[9] Therefore he sins mortally and must restore himself [to his owner], not only because he is a stolen thing but also because of the injustice of running away. It is confirmed that he sins mortally even after going beyond the boundaries of the captor's [territory] when fleeing to his

---

7. Accursius, *Glossa in Digestum Vetus*, Dig. 5.1. at 5.

8. Juan de Torquemada, *In Gratiani decretorum, tomus primum* (Venice: Scoti, 1578), d. 1, a. 4–5 at 47; Antonino of Firenze, *Summa theologica* (Verona: Typographia Seminarii apud Augustinum Crattonium, 1740), part 3, tit. 3, n. 4 at cols. 197–98; Fortunio García de Ercilla y Arteaga, *Commentaria super titulo de justicia et iure* in *De ultimo fine juris canonici et civilis* (Bologna: Ruberiense, 1517), fol. 60, col. 85. Martín de Azpilcueta's seminal work was reprinted numerous times in Portuguese, Latin, and Spanish in the 16th and 17th centuries. Molina might have used the following Latin edition: *Enchiridion sive Manuale Confessariorum* (Roma: Ferrari, 1584), c. 17 n. 103–4 at 383–84.

9. Cod. 6.1.1.

people, because law 3 of the same title established that the person captured during his escape may be punished by having both legs cut off or by being forced into labor in the mines. Such a grave punishment could not be established unless it were for a mortal sin. In truth, on this matter the laws of the *Codex* have more force than the *Digest*, not only because it is posterior but also because it was laid down by Christian princes who established the principles of justice that must be upheld in wars between Christians. It is also an accepted custom that runaway slaves are more severely punished when they are caught fleeing to their people, no matter by what just title they were reduced to slavery. Moreover, if there is no right to punish slaves who were captured in a just war when they flee to join their people, then their slavery is rendered useless. The slaves would continually try to run away, knowing that they would not sin and that they could not be licitly punished for their escape. The owner would have to invest more in searching for them and bringing them back than he gets from their service and their value. Moreover, this mode of slavery would give occasion to many sins by the owners, who would not be able to contain themselves while seeing the slaves continually escaping and they would punish them for the damages caused. For that reason, men would rather justly kill their enemies in war than reduce them to that kind of slavery, which would be to the detriment of those slaves. Consequently, it would be hard to believe that such slavery would have been introduced by the law of nations.

Second, if the contrary view were true [defended by Covarrubias and others], then the slaves we are talking about would become free the moment they cross the boundaries of their captor's territory whether they reach their own people or strangers. It is clear that the authors holding this contrary opinion argued that they [the slaves] do not obtain their freedom because they reach their people but rather because they leave the borders of those who possess them, for indeed it would be absurd [to hold] that Turks captured by the Portuguese who flee to reach the Kingdom of Morocco would not obtain their freedom but instead would be obliged in conscience either to return to their owner to remain in slavery or to go to their own people. And if we follow the literal meaning of what they say, it follows that the Turks or the Africans possessed by the Portuguese under the law of war, when they leave the borders of the Kingdom of Portugal and enter the Kingdom of Castile, especially when these two kingdoms have two different kings, obtain their freedom and are not to be restored to the Portuguese king. It follows that in the Kingdom of Castile they cannot be captured or, if they are justly captured because the Castilians have a just title of war against them, the captors have no obligation to restore them to the Portuguese king. The contrary, however, is the accepted custom.

(11) Third, it is considered that the person captured in a just war and therefore subjected to slavery is by that very fact justly condemned to perpetual slavery and that the captor or the person to whom the captor transfers him truly acquires ownership over him. Now, a person justly condemned to a punishment that he must execute and apply himself is obliged in the court of conscience to do so. Therefore, the captive who finds himself in this situation cannot avoid this slavery by fleeing to his people, and, if he does so, he is obliged to restore himself to the ones he fled from. Slavery is a perpetual punishment that the slave must execute and apply himself. This is evident because, as said above, slavery and exile have the same rationale. And, also, because, if he does not cross the borders of the possessor's territory, he is obliged to execute the punishment himself, as even our adversaries affirm, and ultimately because the person legitimately subjected to slavery under any other title is obliged to execute [the punishment] himself and may not escape.

From this it is clear that the one who persuades a man captured in a just war to escape or helps him escape must compensate the owner for the value of the slave and any pursuant damages if there are any.

(12) From this conclusion is to be excluded the case of the Christian who is justly captured by infidels and who, having fled, cannot return to live with his captors without considerable spiritual harm. In this case, it is sufficient if he gives due compensation [to the captors] in money or some other means because he must not be obliged to return with such spiritual danger to himself. Especially if we consider that their appalling customs are a great occasion for spiritual detriment. Because, if he is forced by the infidels to do evil or is subject to some other injustice, for example, if he is circumcised by Jews or Saracens, he can flee as a just compensation and because there is no one among them to vindicate his right in the face of such wrong, given that it is

to be presumed that this is the will of the prince of his republic or the pontiff, who is the superior and the prince of the republic of the Church and who is in charge of avenging harms to the spiritual good and the Christian religion. To show this, Navarrus and some others cite the chapter *Nulla*, distinction 54.[10] But that chapter refers only to the infidels who live among Christians and who are under their laws and jurisdiction and says nothing about the infidels who are not subject to the laws of a Christian republic.

(13) Second conclusion: When [one side's cause for] war is not so obviously just that the other side cannot, at least formally, fight justly, and particularly considering its subjects who, when in doubt, must obey the king, then when a subject is taken captive in such as just war, although he may be justly detained and coerced so that he does not escape and may be taken back by force if he flees, he may, however, licitly flee to his people or wherever he pleases and has no duty to restore himself. It is proved because in that event the condition of the captured and his owners is equal in that the slave does not have less ownership over himself and possession of his freedom than does his owner, because the war is formally just on both sides. Therefore, he can rightfully withdraw himself from slavery and flee whenever he wishes, especially when he was subjected to slavery by force and the possession began with violence.

(14) Concerning the law *Nihil interest*, from which Covarrubias draws, and some other clearer texts from the Imperial Law that he could have cited, among which is section *Item ea quae ex hostibus. Institut. De rerum divisione*, where it says: "A slave that we capture in a just war by the law of nations is ours: if however he evades our possession and returns to his people, he recovers his original status."[11] We say that this law does not apply when the war of the opposing party is evidently unjust and that it is generally effective only in the court of conscience in the case of our second conclusion and only in the sense that the slave may protect himself, although not presupposing that the owner cannot subject him to slavery, nor does the court of law apply to wars among Christians, as was said in disputation 35, first doubt, before the

10. Cod. 6.1.3.
11. Inst. 2.1.17.

fourth conclusion. According to what has been said here and has been repeated on the matter of war, we may not follow the Imperial Law in itself. Particularly taking into account that the Turks and other Muslims who wage a most unjust war against us judge that the war on their part is just. That is, that in their view any captive obtains his freedom as soon as he leaves our borders, especially if he reaches his people or their allies. And in view of this, the Romans seem to have established these laws. With respect to the laws of Castile that clearly deal with the case in which the war is openly unjust on the side of the adversary and just on our side, it has to be said that the authors followed the Imperial Law on this point and they did not intend to constitute a new positive law in that kingdom.[12] For that reason [these laws] should not be obeyed in the court of conscience nor in the court of law, nor should the Imperial Law be followed on this point, except in the eventuality that the Saracens are offended and prevented from trading and conducting commerce with our people or if they were to do the same with our people, who, having once been their captives and having escaped from their hands, would return [to Saracen lands] to engage in trade or something else during a time of peace.

(15) The provisions of this kingdom about those who capture slaves who run away, the prize that they have a right to, and the punishments that are imposed on them if they do not communicate this to the owner within fifteen days can be seen in book 5 of the *Ordenanzas*, title 41.[13]

12. The implication here is that Castilian laws establish the same rules as Imperial Laws on the matter of captives, but unlike Imperial Laws do so for cases in which only one of the sides can credibly attribute to himself a just cause.

13. In fact, this is a reference to the Law of the Kingdom of Portugal: *Ordenações do reyno de Portugal* (Lisbon: Joam, 1565), lib. 5, tit. 41, at fol. XXXIIIb.

Disputation 38

≈

How far the rights of owners of slaves extend and whether slaves can own something

Summary

1. According to our laws, we can licitly mutilate and kill cattle.

2. What rights over slaves, their labor, and their goods are we given and what [rights] we are denied.

3. How slaves are protected against the cruelty and injustice of their owners.

4. The owners cannot prohibit marriage among slaves.

5. Five cases [that show how] slaves acquire [something] not for their owner but for themselves.

(1) The ownership of slaves does not confer the owners as far-reaching a right over the slaves as does the ownership of cattle, which we can, according to our law, mutilate and even rightfully kill. (2) They [the owners] are conferred rights over all their [the slaves'] work, in keeping with what right reason demands, to be performed according to each's condition and strength; also over all fruits that come from them, such as the children of female slaves and other emoluments, which they [the owners] can properly exact to the point that, if they [the slaves] were to receive a donation or inheritance or if they were to receive something without a will or for any other reason, they would not receive it for

themselves but for their owners according to the civil laws, such as
section 1 of the *Institutions, De iis qui sunt sui vel alieni iuris*, and many
other laws.[1] This has to be understood with the limitations that we will
add. It has been introduced by the law of nations that those captured in
a just war may be subjected to slavery, thus compassionately commuting their temporal death to perpetual slavery. Because of this, slavery
could be understood—as in fact it has been understood, as is evident
from civil laws and from custom itself—in such way that the ownership of slaves encompasses all those rights. The remaining [types] of
slavery, which begin with a title of purchase or with the punishment
for a crime, came into existence later and they are like the ones first
introduced and are to be understood in the same way, unless there were
an exception made by some civil law, such as the one [that states] that
a father can sell his child, which rightly is milder than the other [types
of slavery].

Although the rights of the slave owners appear to be so broad, they
do not, however, encompass their [the slaves'] lives, the ownership of
which is reserved to God; neither do they [encompass] the limbs and
health of the slaves, which are part of their lives and on which their
lives depend. Much less do they encompass their spiritual well-being
in the sense of prescribing or demanding from them something that
would contradict their spiritual well-being. (3) Therefore, if owners
take the life or limbs from a slave or if owners exceed their coactive
power over the slaves through excessive labor, malnourishment, naked-
ness, unjust chastening, or some other unwarranted reason, damaging
their [the slaves'] health or body or commanding anything that goes
against their spiritual health or inflicting on them any other kind of injustice, then they [the owners] would sin mortally if the injustice, considering the condition of the person or the concurring circumstances,
were significant. They would be obliged to make restitution to these
slaves or their heirs for the damages done and they should be punished
by a public authority not only for the unjust damages done to them
[the slaves] but also for those injustices that do not qualify as damages.
On account of these aggressions, their confessors should impose an

---

1. Inst. 1.8.

adequate satisfaction for the slaves, when this injustice has not been punished by a public authority, so that these wretched people would not be deprived of any support after suffering damages and aggressions that they have unjustly received from their owners. Also, the damage or injustice can sometimes be so great that the compensation cannot be anything less than freedom. Lesser damages or injustices, which are neither punished nor heard by a court of law, can be compensated by somewhat reducing the workload, which otherwise would justly have been imposed, giving them better food and clothes, or condoning any wrongdoing for which they could licitly be punished and other such causes [for which they could be licitly punished]. Although the slaves are not allowed to declare against their owner in trial, except in the matter of their freedom and some other eventualities that concern the common good, as is evident in the law *Vix* added to the gloss following *De iudiciis*, they are nonetheless allowed to appear before a judge to denounce injustices and damages that they have received from their owner.[2] The judge is instructed to proceed immediately ex officio to inquire the truth of the accusation and to protect the slaves from the injustice, as is shown in *Institutions, De iis qui sunt sui vel alieni iuris*, last section, and law I, section *Servos*, and section *Quod autem*, and following paragraphs *De officio praefecti urbis*.[3] Panormitanus adds in the chapter *Novit, de iudiciis*, number 48, that those charges do not necessarily require a preceding admonition [to the owner].[4] If an owner kills his slave, he should be punished as a murderer, the same way as if he killed the slave of another person, as stated in *Institutiones, de iis qui sunt sui vel alieni iuris*, where we read the following text: the prince orders "that, if the cruelty of the owners seems to be intolerable, they should be forced to sell their slaves in favorable conditions and the price be given [to the slave] by the owner."[5] And below: "But it is in the owner's interest that help against cruelty, lack of food, and intolerable aggression

---

2. Accursius, *Glossa in Digestum Vetus*, Dig. 5.1.53 at 105b.

3. See Inst. 1.8. Cod. and 1.28.1.1 and Dig. 1.12.7.

4. Nicolò dei Tudeschi (Panormitanus), *Commentaria super prima parte secundi libri decretalium* (Turin: Bevilaquae, 1577), tit. 1 (*De iudiciis*), chap. 13 (*Novit ille*), n. 48 at 36a.

5. Inst. 1.8.2.

should not be denied. Therefore, you [the judge] should acknowledge their grievances and, if they are treated harsher than is fair, which is the same, or if you came to know that they were subjected to infamous injustices, they should be forced to be sold so as not to return under the power of their owner."[6] And in the law 1, section *Quod autem, De officio praefecti urbis* it is stated: "If the owners mistreat the slaves with cruelty, harshness, and hunger, if they have been forced or are being forced into lewdness, they [the slaves] should expose that to the prefect of the town."[7] And the law *Si lenones*, codex, *De episcopali audientia*, establishes that, if the owners impose on their female slaves the necessity to sin, the bishops can free them from slavery and give them their freedom in order to punish the crimes of their owners.[8] With good reason Saint Antoninus in part 3, title 3, chapter 6, section 7, states that, if an owner were to demand his slave to sin, he could rightfully flee from his owner when he [the owner], having been admonished, does not desist. One might add that he [the slave] has no obligation to return unless the danger has disappeared and if the owner does not wish to punish or to fine him because of that event and cause. Since the owner was to blame, the slave had a just cause to flee and he did not deserve any punishment. Exodus 21 confirms this: "He that strikes his bondman or bondwoman with a rod, and they die under his hands, shall be guilty of the crime."[9] And below: "If any man strikes the eye of his manservant or maidservant and leave them but one eye, he shall let them go free for the eye he put out. Also, if he strikes out a tooth of his manservant or maidservant, he shall in like manner make them free."[10] Even though those judicial laws ceased [to be effective], they were based on equity (*aequitate*). Today natural law obliges those who commit similar crimes against their slaves to give those slaves adequate satisfaction, because [the slaves] are human beings and neighbors and because the harm and injustice done to them is beyond the power of their owners. Hence Tostado rightfully notes, regarding that passage of question 27, that if

6. Inst. 1.8.2.

7. Dig. 1.12.7.

8. Cod. 1.4.12.

9. Ex 21:20.

10. Ex 21:26–27.

someone were to kill the slave of another person or if he were to beat him in such a way as to render him unable for service or diminish his value, he [the owner] is obliged to twofold restitution: one to the owner of the slave, because he has been damaged, and another to the slave because of the damage he received.[11] At the same time he has to be punished by a public authority, which should serve as a compensation for the injustices done to the slave. Therefore, it is obvious that the one who unjustly strikes his own slave sins less than when [striking unjustly] the slave of another person, since [in the first case] damage and injustice are done only to one [person], [in the second case] to two.

(4) Just as the right of slave owners does not extend to that which has been noted above, they cannot forbid them [the slaves] from contracting matrimonial union and its fulfilment either to propagate [human] nature or as a remedy against lust, which is allowed according to natural law and which the law of nations, under which slavery was introduced, could not abolish or prevent. For this reason, the owners cannot prohibit their slaves from contracting marriage, as is established in chapter 1 of *De coniugio servorum* and elsewhere.[12] And should they forbid it, they would be doing an injustice, and they [the slaves] can marry against the will of the owners and be protected and defended against them by the Church. This [I say] as concerns the first [of the questions] that have been laid out in this disputation.

Regarding the second, it has to be said, as the laws prescribe, that whatever they [the slaves] regularly acquire, they purchase for their owners, yet in the following cases they purchase something for themselves and acquire true ownership.

(5) The first case: If there is a pact between them and the owner so that they pay him [the owner] on a daily, weekly, monthly, or yearly basis but keep the rest of their labor and profits for themselves or if there is a similar pact, which very frequently is the case in this Kingdom of Portugal and which has become customary. This is why many slaves redeem themselves with their own money. Although the owner's relationship with the slave, inasmuch as he is a slave, is not one of

11. Alfonso del Madrigal (Tostado), *Commentaria in Primam partem Exodi* (Venice: Balleoniana, 1728) in Ex 21:27 at 362–63.

12. X.4.9.

friendship or justice, both [that is, friendship and justice] can be the case, however, inasmuch as he is a human being, as Aristotle states in book 8, chapter 13, of the *Ethics*.[13] Therefore, the owner has to respect the contract and he cannot seize the things the slave has acquired for himself in this way.

The second case: When an owner tacitly or openly gives something to his slave or if he wants the slave to have it as his own either through donation, gambling, or any other reason. If there can be a contract between an owner and a slave, not inasmuch as he is a slave but because he is a human being who happens to be a slave, as has just been said, then there can be a donation; and, after the first time the owner has done it freely, it cannot be revoked unless there is a just cause. Hence, those things have to be distinguished that the owner tacitly or openly gives to the slave, that is, whether they are given only to be used or whether they belong to the slave to be freely at his disposal. In the former case, the slave does not acquire ownership; in the latter, however, he acquires it.

The third case: When the owner or someone else restores something to the slave because of a damage or an injustice in matters that are not subject to the owner's power according to what was said above. Since the restitution is due to an injustice done to him inasmuch as he is a human being and with regard to those things that are beyond the owner's power, he truly acquires ownership of those things.

The fourth case: When something is given or entrusted to him on the tacit or explicit condition that it belongs to the slave and not to the owner. Even if the father has the usufruct of adventitious goods, if they have been given to the son on the condition that the usufruct belongs to him and not to the father, the son acquires the usufruct of the thing for himself, as has been said in distinction 8.[14] Hence, if something has

13. The text referred to is actually book 8, chap. 11. Aristotle, *Nicomachean Ethics* 1161b8-11.

14. According to the *Real Diccionario de la Academia*: "An adventitious good is a good acquired by the son of a family through his work in some trade, art, or industry or by fortune, donation, or inheritance while under paternal authority (*patria potestad*)." The *Partidas* established that the ownership of these goods belongs to the son and the usufruct to the father while under the *patria potestad. Partidas* 4, 5, and 17 and *Leyes de Toro* 47 and 48.

been given to the slave by that law so that it is his but not his owner's, then the owner truly does not own it and he [the slave] can do with his own things as he wishes and he can set the conditions under which they [the goods] can be obtained by this or that [person]. Consequently, in that case the ownership of that good does not belong to the owner [of the slave] but rather to the slave. Something would be relinquished with the tacit condition that it belongs to the slave and not to the owner, if, for example, it were said: "I relinquish or give to the slave of Peter an amount so that he may redeem himself."

The fifth case: When he [the slave] makes a profit with the goods of which he is the owner, by gambling or in any other business, without any prejudice to the services that he owes to the owner, the profits end up being his.

All these [cases] do not contradict Imperial Law; rather they support it by teaching as evident that slaves may occasionally possess their own goods and that they may celebrate with their goods a valid contract with their [the slaves'] owners. Law 1, section *Servos, De officio praefecti urbi*, [listing] the cases to which it applies, says the following words: "Those slaves who have been bought with their own money to be freed should be listened to when they complain about their owners."[15] And the law *Vix de iudiciis*, among other cases that allow slaves to initiate court proceedings against their owners, includes one with these words: "Yet if [the slaves] state that they have redeemed themselves with their own coin and yet have not been freed despite the pledge given."[16] Therefore, the laws that state that slaves do not acquire [anything] for themselves but only for their owners have to be understood considering normal conditions and when nothing contrary is evident. About the contracts of legal slaves, more will be said in disputation 261.

15. Dig. 1.12.7.
16. Dig. 1.12.8

Disputation 39

Ways to free slaves from slavery

Summary

1. Nine ways for a slave to abandon slavery.

Something has to be said about the ways of freeing slaves from slavery. The first and most common is to set them free either gratuitously or after paying a price or levying a charge or some similar reason.

The second: When an owner or anyone else abandons a child knowingly or without opposition or when he did not know that he had been abandoned and approved of it after the fact; by that very reason, such a child remains free. Similarly, when an owner abandons a sick slave or when he denies him the necessary food, then the slave is considered abandoned and thus obtains his freedom. Nor does anyone who takes him [the slave] in and takes care of him acquire a right [of property] over such a slave. These [cases] are defined in the only chapter, *De infantibus et languidis expositis*, laws 2 and 3, [and] in the codex with the same title, last law, *Pro derelicto*, and the sole law section *Sed scimus*, codex *De latina libertate tollenda*.[1]

The third: When an owner forces a female slave to fornicate, she is absolved of all the necessity of her misery after imploring the help of the bishop, as is stated in the law *Si lenones*, codex *De episcopali audientia*.[2] The gloss, however, says on this text that everyone has always

---

1. X.11.1, actually Dig. 41.7. Also Cod. 7.6.1.
2. That is, the coerced sexual relationship. Cod. 1.4.12.

understood this law to mean that the bishop should give her freedom.[3]

The fourth: When a Jew, a pagan, or a heretic possesses with some kind of title a slave who is already Christian. For this very reason that slave acquires his freedom without [having] to pay a price. If he [a Jew, a pagan, or a heretic] possesses a slave who is not yet Christian and if that slave wishes to be baptized, then, after becoming a Christian, he acquires his freedom in similar fashion; and, even if the owner receives the faith later, the slave does not forfeit his freedom because of this. This is stated in the law *Deo nobis*, section *his ita*, codex *De episcopis et cleris*.[4] Furthermore, this sanction and others of this kind, which will be discussed [below], are to be applied to those infidels, who are subject to the temporal jurisdiction of the Church and its members, because they live in lands under the jurisdiction of the Church. These infidels, by virtue of the temporal jurisdiction exerted over them, are deservedly forbidden to initiate [the possession] of slaves who are already Christians. The condition is rightly imposed on them that if they wish to possess another [slave], he [the slave] can be legally possessed only if he were to obtain his freedom without paying a price should he convert to the [Christian] faith. Infidels, who are not subject to the temporal jurisdiction of the Church, cannot be forbidden to possess a Christian slave nor can any condition be imposed upon them in this respect. Gregory IX later established in the last chapter of *De Iudaeis et Saracenis* that, if a Jew had bought an infidel slave as merchandise and if that slave wished to be baptized, the Jew should receive twelve solidi (that is, a gold coin with the value of fourteen silver reales and nine maravedís, as will be explained below in disputation 278) [and the slave] should remain free.[5] But, if neither the slave nor anyone else in his place could pay, the Jew would be obliged to offer him for sale within three months from the day of his baptism. If he is not put up for sale at the end of these months, the slave remains free without paying any price. If he offers him for sale and there is no Christian to buy him, then the slave may go from door to door begging or he may serve

3. Accursius, *Glossa in Codicem*, Cod. 1.4.12 at 18.

4. Codex. 1.3.54.8.

5. The solidus was a gold coin issued in the Late Roman Empire and Byzantine Empire. The Spanish silver coin real de plata was worth thirty-four maravedís.

the infidel until he is able to sufficiently compensate for the money;
otherwise he should be released so that he may serve someone else
and thus earn money to pay [the owner]. If, however, a Christian were
to buy him within the three prescribed months, he does not become
a permanent slave but only until he has compensated the money that
was paid for him. He [the Christian owner] does not acquire a greater
right [of property] over him after he was baptized than the one the Jew
had. This is the meaning of that law. Read the first and second chapters
of the same title, the chapter *Mancipia* and the chapter *Fraternitatem*,
distinction 54.

Two issues should be recalled: The first is that, if the slave has not
been bought as merchandise but is either a home-born slave, that is,
born to a female slave of a Jew, or if he has been purchased for a price
to perform services for him [the owner], then he remains free without
paying a price. Secondly, the arrangement of the last chapter *De Iudaeis*
also applies to the slaves of pagans and Muslims subjected to the temporal jurisdiction of the Church due to the parity of reasons and because
of what I will now add.

The fifth: When a Jew has circumcised his infidel slave. As a punishment for this crime, he [the slave] remains free. This is what the only
law of the codex *Ne Christianum mancipium* states. I believe that the
same is true today if a Muslim subject to the temporal jurisdiction of
the Church circumcises his pagan slave. I am led [to this opinion], because, on the one hand, the same reason applies and, on the other hand,
because without mentioning pagans or heretics, shortly before [the law
Ne Christianum mancipium] a law had been established [stating] that,
should a Jew possess a Christian slave, his slave should remain free.
The law *Deo nobis*, section *His ita*, codex *De episcopis et cleris*, referring
to the emperor in the sole law in the Codex's section *Ne Christianum
mancipium*, says: "Recurring to that law we command that no Jew or
pagan or heretic should have Christian slaves; should they be found
in such state of guilt, we decree that the slaves shall be free in every
way according to the purpose of our older laws. In the present case we
further decree ..., etc.," [says] this emperor.[6] As you can see, what he

6. Codex 1.3.54.8 and codex 1.10.

said about the Jewish people he wanted to be understood [also] about heretics and pagans. For the same reason, today both laws have to be applied to Muslims who were not then included under the designation of pagans or heretics. If a Jew were to circumcise his slave, he [the slave] would immediately acquire his freedom, which has been sanctioned by Canon Law in the Third Council of Toledo, chapter 14, which refers to the chapter *Nulla*, dist. 54, and in the Fourth Council of Toledo, chapter 57, which is stated in *De consecratione*, dist. 4, chapter *Plerique*.[7] What we said about this fifth way in which a slave obtains his freedom, as well as what has been said about the fourth way, applies frequently to the infidels of the Eastern Indies [Asia] who are subject to the jurisdiction of the Christians.

Sixth: When an unmarried man takes his handmaid as his concubine and continues living with her in such way that it [the concubinate] lasts until [his] death. Although the handmaid as well as her children—if he has fathered them with her—remain slaves as long as he lives, they completely remain slaves after his death if he transfers them to someone or if he declares that they should remain as slaves of the heir. If he does not pronounce anything with respect to them, then by the time of the owner's death the handmaid and her children—assuming he fathered them with her—remain free based on the same right. This much is stated in the last law of the codex *Communia de manumissionibus*. The *Ordinationes* of the Portuguese kingdom book 4, title 71,[8] at the beginning do not contradict this, because, after it has been established that the natural children of a plebeian, that is, a *piaon*, should succeed their father as if they were legitimate, it is added that the same should be said of the child who has been born to such a *piaon* and his handmaid, assuming that by the time of death of such a father the child remains free.[9] It is clear that this privilege does not apply when the handmaid's owner was a clergyman or a married man or when some-

7. On Fourth Council of Toledo, chap. 14 and chap. 56, *Concilios visigóticos e hispano-romanos*, ed. José Vives (Madrid and Barcelona: CSIC and Instituto Enrique Flórez, 1963), at 129 and at 214.

8. *Ordenações do reyno de Portugal* (Lisbon: Joam, 1565), lib. 4, tit. 71 at fol. 52.

9. The term *piaon* reflects the Portuguese term *piam* (modern *peão*), originally designating non-noble footmen; see *DIEI* II.166, col.939c–d.

thing else prevented him from marrying her. Furthermore, if a man has had his handmaid as a concubine for some time, but has not kept her any longer as a concubine, because he has taken a wife or for some other reason, then that handmaid does not enjoy this privilege, even if she has given birth to a child with her owner, which can be clearly deduced from this law. As for the children born to her it has to be said that they enjoy this privilege. I leave it to the jurists to determine to what extent this was accepted by custom. You always have to lean toward freedom, especially that of the children who are born without any guilt of their own. Covarrubias in his epitome to the fourth decree, part 2, section 7, deduces from the *Authenticum, De triente et semisse* in the last paragraph, that, even if the owner of such a handmaid were to marry her later, neither she nor the children born to her would obtain freedom, but they could only enjoy the privilege [established] by the last law of the codex *Communia de manumissionibus.*[10] If, however, only the mother has been set free, then her children would hence remain free. In the Kingdom of Castile, the very fact that the owner married the handmaid implies that she, as well as the children born to her, would obtain their freedom according to the first law, title 13, and the fifth law, *Partida* 4, of the laws of Castile.[11]

Seventh: If a free person marries a slave without knowing of her slavery and if the owner either gives her in marriage without disclosing her slavery or, knowing that both are to be married, does not disclose [her slavery], that person who is a slave, whether male or female, obtains by this very fact [his or her] freedom. This can be established from the *Authenticum,* chapter *De nuptiis,* section *Si vero ab initio,* and first law, title 5, part 4, of the laws of Castile and that are transmitted by the last gloss and by the jurists [commenting] on the last and first chapter *De coniugio servorum.*[12] Covarrubias confirms this in the aforementioned

10. Diego Covarrubias y Leyva, *In quartum decretalium librum epitome* (Lyon: Juntae, 1558), pars 7, cap. noted as *septimus* (it is actually the fourth) at 55b.

11. *Quarta partida* (Valladolid: Diego Férnandez de Córdoba, 1587), tit. 13, ley 1 at fol. 39b; tit. 22, ley 5 at fol. 57b.

12. Accursius, *Glossa in Volumen Corpus Glossatorum Juris Civilis*, ed. Mario Viora (Turin: Officina Erasmiana, 1969) vol. 11. This is the gloss to *Authenticum* in col. 4.1 at 32.

text, as well as in Álvaro Velasco's *De iure emphyteutico*, question 36, numbers 4 and 5.[13] Also, if someone gives his handmaid in marriage to a free man who does not ignore her slavery but provides a written instrument concerning the dowry in favor of the handmaid, this will immediately result in her freedom, as is shown in the only law, section *Sed et si quis homini*, and the corresponding *Authenticum*, codex *De latina libertate tollenda*, which Covarrubias and Álvaro Velasco corroborate in the cited place.[14] From this the following is clear: When both parts who contract marriage are slaves or when one is free but does not ignore the slavery of the other, he does not obtain his freedom, even if the owner has expressly agreed to the marriage, as long as a written instrument concerning the handmaid's dowry has not been provided. As Velasco observes, the common people make this mistake [of believing that freedom is obtained without the instrument].

Eighth: If someone declares his slave to be his heir or his child's tutor without ignoring that he is his slave. In both cases, by this very fact, it is considered that he has conceded his freedom, as will be shown below in disputation 154.

Ninth: If someone adopts his slave as his child. He [the slave] immediately obtains his freedom as is shown in the last paragraph of the *Instituta, De adoptionibus*, and at the end of our disputation 227.[15]

13. Álvaro Velasco, *Tractatus de iure emphyteutico* (Cremona: Pellizari, 1591), q. 36, n. 4–5 at fol. 214b–215a.

14. The dowry referred to in this passage is called *dotis instrumentum*: a notarial prenuptial agreement that takes into account the fact that the handmaid does not have the means to offer a dowry of her own. Also Codex 7.6.1.9. Gustavus Ernestus Heimbach, ed., *Authenticum: Novellarum Constitutionum Iustiniani* (Leipzig: Barth, 1851), novella 22, cap. 10 at 216 and cap. 17 at 223.

15. Inst. 1.11.12.

Disputation 40

Whether Christian slaves that belong to those
condemned by the Inquisition of the crime
of heresy or apostasy remain free

Summary

1. Slaves that belong to heretics or apostates condemned by the court of the Inquisition are free according to Common Law and the laws of Castile if they were Christians at the time their owners committed their crimes. On what applies in Portugal.
2. Response to the basic assumptions of the author.
3. Rejection.
4. Response to other basic assumptions of the author.
5. Rejection.
6. Response to the Canon Law quoted by the author.
7. Rejection.
8. Response to the last chapter of *De haereticis*.
9. Satisfactory response.
10. Response to the contrary point of view.
11. Another point of view, which is equally rejected.

Notwithstanding the preceding disputation on the fourth way by which slaves may obtain their freedom, [where it is said that] it is generally clear that Christian slaves of heretics and other infidels, who are under the temporal jurisdiction of the Church, obtain *eo ipso* their freedom, there is the peculiar difficulty as to whether the same can be said of Christian slaves of heretics and apostates who have been condemned by a court of the Inquisition.

(1) Alfonso de Castro in book 2 *of De iusta haereticorum punitione*, chapter 7; Jacobo Simancas in *De catholicis institutionibus*, title 61, number 8; and Francisco Peña in *Ad tertiam partem directorii*, question 119, commentary 168, think that the affirmative part is true and that it is an established custom in Castile.[1] Francisco Peña also quotes a decree of the first Spanish instruction that had been approved by the Catholic monarchs Ferdinand and Isabella and that established that slaves who are already Christians and who are found among the possessions of heretics and apostates should not be given to the treasury; rather they should be granted their freedom.[2] Therefore, Simancas and Francisco Peña say that, if one of those heretics were to return to the unity of the Church within a period of grace, thus receiving [back] all the goods that had been given to the king, his Christian slaves should nonetheless obtain their freedom, which they had acquired because of the crimes of their owners.

Staying within the Common Law [*ius commune*], the Imperial Law, or the Church Law, to me this stance has always seemed to be true. Beginning with the Imperial Law, to start with the most ancient one, one can be convinced, first, by the only law of the codex *Ne Christianum mancipium* and from the book *Deo nobis,* section *his autem*, codex *De episcopis et cleris*.[3] These legal texts decree (as has been shown and deduced in the previous fourth, fifth, and sixth ways with regard to how

---

1. Alfonso de Castro, *De iusta haereticorum punitione: libri tres* (Antwerp: Widow and Sons of Stelfius, 1568), lib. 2., cap. 7 at 160–62; Diego de Simancas, *De catholicis institutionibus* (Rome: Aedibus Populi Romani, 1575), tit. 61, n. 8 at 457 (Jacobo Simancas and Diego de Simancas are the same person); Francisco Peña, *Flores commentariorum reverendissimi d. Francisci Pegnae in Directorium inquisitorum* (Milano: Bordonum, 1610), 210; Nicholas Eymerich, *Directorium inquisitorum cum commentariis Francisci Pegnae* (Rome: Aedibus Populi Romani, 1587), pars. 3, q. 119, comm. 168, 675–76.

2. *Compilación de las Instrucciones del Oficio de la Santa Inquisición hechas por el muy Reverendo Señor Fray Tomás de Torquemada* (Madrid: Diego Díaz de la Carrera, 1667), chap. 24 at 8.

3. Cod. 1.10; Cod. 1.3.54.8.

slaves obtain their freedom) that a Christian slave who belongs to Jews, pagans, or heretics shall obtain his freedom. This applies also to an infidel slave who wishes to convert to the Christian faith, because, when they [the slaves] are baptized, they immediately receive their freedom, which they do not lose if afterward their owner becomes a Christian. But as soon as a Christian commits heresy and apostasy of the faith, it is true to say that the Christian slaves he already possessed or those who by whatever title came to be in his possession while he was committing the crime [of heresy] are slaves of a heretic. Hence, by the force of the law we have quoted, they obtain their freedom. Since those laws that at a later point in time decreed the proscription of the heretic's goods did not abrogate these earlier laws nor have they been introduced to enrich the treasury [*fiscus*] to the detriment of the freedom of Christian slaves but only to eliminate the heresy by the severity of the punishment without having a reason to contradict those earlier laws—because the law of confiscation only gives to the treasury the possessions of the heretics, who, without that law, would have remained in possession of those goods after having committed the crime—and among those goods there are no Christian slaves, who by virtue of the previous law were freed at the time of the first heresy,[4] it follows that, remaining within the limit of Imperial Law and Canon Law, the Christian slaves of those heretics or apostates who have been convicted of the crime of heresy by a court of the Inquisition are free and they do not belong to the king's treasury.

Second: The law *Manicheos*, codex *De haereticis*, which, among other punishments, was enacted to transfer the goods of heretics to the treasury without their children having access to the paternal inheritance (unless they embrace the Catholic faith after repudiating their error) and which grants to the infidel slaves of the heretics that they may remain free if they convert to the Catholic faith.[5] Hence, the fact that heretics are to be punished by means of the confiscation of their goods does not deny that their Christian slaves obtain their freedom

---

4. Proscription of goods in this context means that the property of heretics is transferred to the treasury of the crown or realm, assuming that the heretic has been convicted by the Inquisition.

5. Cod. 1.5.4.

by virtue of the former laws without having to transfer them to the treasury with the rest of the heretic's goods.

Third: According to Canon Law, chapter 1, and more clearly in chapter 2 and in the last chapter of *De Iudaeis et Saracenis* and in the chapters *Mancipia* and *Fraternitatem*, distinction 54, the Christian slaves of Jews who are subject to the temporal jurisdiction of the Church are automatically free.[6] But the heretics whose apostasy leads them to Judaism (who in Spain own almost all the slaves we are talking about) are true Jews who belong to the temporal and spiritual jurisdiction of the Church, even though they have been baptized, and hence they are apostates of the faith. Therefore, since it has been established in the first argument that the law of confiscation refers only to those goods that, without this law, would continue to belong to the apostate at the time of the crime of heresy and apostasy and that [this law] was not made to enrich the treasury but rather to punish the heretics, these slaves would remain free and would not belong to the treasury.

Fourth: In the last chapter of *De haereticis*, Gregory IX says he is absolved "of owing loyalty to the owners" (the new edition says "men") "and of all duties, whoever is related to those who manifestly lapse into heresy by means of an agreement in whatever way it has been thought to be binding" (those are the words found in the text).[7] Hence the slaves of heretics and even of apostates from the Catholic faith, by the very fact that the crime of their owners is manifest, become free, and therefore they do not belong to the treasury. This reasoning is corroborated by the chapter *Quicumque*, section *Illorum autem, de haereticis*, book 6, where Alexander IV declares that the emancipation of the heretic's children after the crime has been committed by the father is null and void, even if after their emancipation it becomes clear that they were heretics while completing it [the emancipation].[8] The pope adds the argument that such emancipation is achieved "by men who were already legally independent (*sui iuris*), because it is," as he notes, "appropriate that due to the atrocity of the crime the children cease to be under the tutelage of their heretic parents," as the text states. And, even if the

6. X.5.6. 1, 2 and D. 54, caps. 13 and 15.

7. X.5.7.16.

8. VI.5.2.2.

children do not become legally independent because of the crimes of the father even if there has been evidence of those crimes, but [become independent] only according to the provision of Gregory IX, in the last chapter of the quoted text, all those who were subject to him are eo ipso released from the oath of fidelity to their owner and, consequently, also Christian slaves, when the owner commits the crime of heresy, eo ipso become legally independent and they remain free and do not belong to the treasury.

But John Andreae, Francus, Geminianus and Perusinus in the chapter *Quicumque*, section *illorum, de haereticis,* book 6, and John of Anania and Marianus Socinus in the last chapter in the book *Extra* thought that the slaves of those who were condemned for heresy and apostasy may not obtain their freedom but that they belong to the treasury instead, as do the goods of those heretics.[9] Their teaching is based on no other reason than comparing the subjugation of the slaves of a heretic after a crime has been committed with the emancipation of his child that occurred at the same time. They assert that the emancipation was void because it concerned a man who was already legally independent because of the crimes of his father, as is said in section *Illorum,* whereas the manumission is void, not for that reason, but because the heretic already lacked ownership of his slave, who by the same law was confiscated along with the goods belonging to the heretic, according to the chapter *Cum secundum leges, de haereticis*, book 6.

Francisco Peña, however, says of these jurists that they speak only of those slaves who have not yet become Christians. Since they do not acquire their freedom according to either Imperial Law or Canon Law, they clearly belong to the treasury, as do the remaining goods of the heretic. If they [the jurists] were to understand this of the Christians, then one should not listen to their assertion because it is not based on the solid ground of Imperial or Canon Law, which establishes the contrary and which would satisfy them if they bore it in mind. Moreover, the distinction between Christian and non-Christian slaves was made clear for this very purpose in the quoted instruction of Seville; it says: "The rulers, king and queen, wished to grant freedom to the slaves

---

9. *Liber sextus decretalium* (Lyon, 1584), VI.5.2.2. The glosses can be found in col. 612.

of any heretic, if they [their heretics] have lived under the authority of Christians."[10]

As far as the Portuguese kingdom was concerned, a tribunal of the Inquisition was established during the reign of John III. Yet, it was not until the time of King Sebastian that the goods of those who had been condemned by this tribunal were given to the treasury.[11] The reason for this was that the descendants of Hebrews made a pact with the king that for a certain amount of gold they would obtain [the right to retain their slaves] for a certain number of years.[12] After that time had elapsed and after the confiscation of those goods had begun and judges had been appointed for that purpose, doubts arose as to whether the Christian slaves of those men, who were not few in that kingdom, should remain free or whether they should belong to the treasury. Since, up to that time, the goods of those people were given to them or to their [Jewish] heirs in the absence of a will, according to the covenant mentioned, no one thought about the matter of those wretched slaves, and so they were given to their owners along with the rest of the goods.[13] But when some learned men met to judge this and other doubtful matters, there existed no law in this kingdom that could overrule previous ones. Nor existed any precepts based on custom ([a custom] that could not have taken root in the lapse of time from the inception of the tribunal of the Inquisition in this kingdom until now and especially because it would have contradicted Canon Law and freedom) stating that these slaves could not remain free and that they should rather belong to the king's treasury. If I am not mistaken, they followed [the rules] there for no

10. *Instrucciones del Oficio de la Santa Inquisición*, chap. 24 at 8.

11. King John III (1502–57) governed Portugal from 1521 until his death. King Sebastian (1554–78) was crowned in 1557 and governed until his death.

12. A number of decisions by King Manuel I protected the property of converso Jews. In 1512 the king prolonged for sixteen years some of the protection of new Christians from the Inquisition. João Lúcio de Azevedo, *Historia dos Cristãos Novos Portugueses* (Lisbon: Livraria Classica, 1922), 61. Later suspensions of confiscations from new Christians included a suspension for ten years, decreed by King Sebastian in 1580, in exchange for 225,000 cruzados paid by the conversos. See Salvador Alexandre, *Judeus, Cristãos-novos e a inquisição* (Lisbon: Prefacio, 2002), 66–70.

13. The kind of inheritance referred to here is *ab intestato*, which is a legal procedure by which goods are adjudicated to an heir in the absence of a will.

other reasons than those given by those jurists, on whom I have reported, and because their view is generally accepted without producing any dissenting interpretations.

A few years after [those rules] had been given—while commenting at the University of Evora on the *Secunda Secundae* of Saint Thomas on this very disputation that I have presented and having previously discussed our opinion on this matter with some of the inquisitors, who did not dislike our point of view that is based on the tenets of Alfonso de Castro and Jacobo Simancas—we affirmed that, from the point of view of Common Law, the Christian slaves of these men should be free.[14] We add that, if it were considered advantageous, they should not receive their freedom but rather should belong to the treasury, because the hope of freedom might give them an opportunity to accuse their owners of crimes; yet in the future the law can be changed for that reason. This is because the Imperial Laws (as stated in book 2 of the *Ordinationes*, title 5) apply in the kingdom only to the extent that they do not contradict the private laws of the kingdom and the customary precepts.[15] Should a part [of those laws] state something contrary, then they should be abrogated. Referring to Canon Law, this partial abrogation can be obtained from the pope. I have said, however, that slaves who have acquired their freedom by virtue of Imperial and Canon Laws from the time of the erection of the tribunal of the Inquisition to the present time, without recurring to ignorance, are completely free, and there has been no period of time in which [freedom] from slavery would prescribe, as is shown by the codex *De longi temporis praescriptione, quae pro libertate*, taken from the law *Usucapionem*, and the chapter *De usucapionem*, from the paragraph *Sed aliquando*, [as well as from] Institutions *De usucapionibus*, and from book 6, title 29, paragraph 3 of the Laws of Castile.[16] The same has to be said of the children of female slaves and, in general, of those who follow the female line.

Later, there was no lack of attempts to refute our reasons stating that, considering Common Law alone, these slaves were not free at all but rather belonged to the treasury and that no one had ever acquired

14. Aquinas, *Summa Theologiae*, II-II, q. 10, a. 10.

15. *Ordenações do reyno de Portugal*, lib. 2, tit. 5 at fol. vib–vii.

16. Cod. 7.22.3; Inst 2.6.1; *Siete partidas* (1555), vol. 2, partida 3, ley 6 at 166.

his freedom after the erection of the tribunal of the Inquisition in this kingdom.

(2) In order to buttress this opinion, they reply that the law *Deo nobis,* section *His ita,* refers only to heretics who live publicly as heretics and who were allowed to keep their belongings and to have their meeting places, as is allowed today in Germany and France.[17] The reason, however, why it has been decreed that Christian slaves should remain free is that they are in danger of being perverted by the [heretics]. But it is said that the heretics and apostates of whom we are now speaking about are not allowed to live in their error but, after they are discovered, all their belongings and slaves are immediately seized to be given to the treasury after the sentence. It follows that the reason for this law ceases to exist for these slaves and that the heretics to whom this law applies are not covered by it.

(3) In the first place I answer that, as a law has been universally established concerning the Christian slaves of heretics, regardless whether these heretics may be allowed without any restriction to live with their belongings or whether they are subject to more serious punishments consisting in their not being able to live publicly in their error and in not being allowed to enjoy their belongings after their error has been discovered, which have been confiscated by the treasury. Yet the law does not in the least destroy the privilege introduced in favor of the faith and freedom of Christian slaves, which continues to exist in its entirety especially because it promotes the faith, insofar as infidel slaves could hope to be drawn to the faith in the hope of acquiring their freedom. As long as the law does not distinguish or make exceptions [between tolerated and not tolerated heretics], we should not distinguish or make exceptions and, when in doubt, we should follow the words of the law that promote faith and freedom. In this case, I do not see what reason there could be to establish the contrary with certainty, as long as that law is valid. This can be confirmed as follows: If after [promulgating] those laws, further punishments for the heretics were to be forthcoming, even capital punishment, and, if after thorough inquiry the heretics were not allowed to continue living in their error and if only the punishment of

17. Cod. 1.3.54.8.

confiscating their belongings had not been imposed, then there would be no one who would dare to ascertain that the Christian slaves of those heretics should not be freed on the basis of that previous law. Since the law of confiscation was not enacted to increase the wealth of the princes or to diminish the favor and privilege of the faith and freedom but only to coerce and punish the heretics, consequently and without doubt, the Christian slaves of the heretics obtain their freedom even after the enactment of the law of confiscation.

Next we will show, based on Civil Law, that even after the law [dealing with] confiscation and with the seizure by confiscation of Christian slaves who belong to heretics, these slaves obtain their freedom. The law of confiscation was established by Theodosius in the law *Manicheos*, so that the slaves and other goods seized from heretics and given to the treasury could not be given to their children unless they renounced the ungodliness of their fathers and become Catholics. That same law, without confiscation impeding it, conceded freedom to the slaves of the heretics, whose [the heretics] goods were to be confiscated, if they [the slaves] wished to become Catholics. From this it follows, as the same law shows, that [the fact that according to this law] the goods of the heretics were to be given to the treasury and that the slaves were not to remain in the possession of the heretics or their non-Catholic children, did not prevent their complete freedom. After the law *Manicheos*, which was established by Theodosius, Justinian, who succeeded Theodosius, established the law *Deo nobis* that this controversy deals with. [This law] did not in the least abrogate the law of confiscation established by Theodosius but rather presupposed it, as did the single law codex *Ne Christianum mancipium* established by Constantine, referring to section *His ita*, since it says: "Falling back on the law we command, etc." For this reason, what the law has sanctioned must also be understood with regard to the Christian slaves of those heretics whose slaves are to be seized and given to the treasury because of their crime of heresy.

(4) As to the law *Manicheos*, by which we have confirmed our opinion in the second place, [the critic] replies that this first law applies only to the slaves of Manicheans and Donatists, who are the only ones to whom this law refers, but today there are no such [people, that is,

Manicheans and Donatists]. Hence, this law does not grant freedom to slaves, instead it only states that they are not liable to harm (*extra noxa*), if, having escaped from a sacrilegious owner, they join the Catholic church in order to perform a more faithful service. He [the critic] says that, while the words "*extra noxam sint*" of Accursius's gloss mean "to be free," it is often believed that slaves are granted their freedom by this law. However, the word "harm" (*noxa*) in the Latin language never means slavery, implying that someone *extra noxa* is free. Rather, it means either guilt or punishment.[18] Its meaning is to be free from guilt and punishment.

(5) To the first of these arguments it has to be said that, although this law speaks only of Manicheans and Donatists, the same reasons apply to other heretics and that the reasons given in this law for punishing them in this way apply to all [heretics]. Therefore, it has to be understood that this law justifiably has to be extended to all [heretics]. Justinian approaches the law *Deo nobis,* section *his ita,* in such a way that it must be interpreted as referring to all heretics by virtue of this law and that of the single law Cod. *Ne Christianum mancipium* when it states: "Falling back on the law, etc."[19] He himself, in the same paragraph, speaks of all in general.

To the second argument it has to be said that the meaning of this law is obvious and that not only Accursius understood it this way (whose gloss is valid in this kingdom, because it is not rejected by the common opinion of the jurists nor is it contrary to the law or normative precedent, as stated in book 2, title 2, of the *Ordinationes*) but also the common opinion of the jurists [understood it in this way].[20] Accursius in his gloss did not understand the word "harm" as slavery but as guilt and punishment. However, when he explained the word "harm," he very briefly revealed the meaning of the whole sentence: "It is: they will be free." The expression "they will be" is in the future tense and when the sentence is considered, it clearly indicates that it is not only an exposition of the utterance "harm" but of the complete sentence, which is the correct and legitimate meaning. Theodosius clearly states that a

18. Accursius, *Glossa in Codicem*, cod. 1.5.4. at 19b.

19. Cod. 1.10.8.

20. *Ordenações do reyno de Portugal,* lib. 2, tit. 5 at fol. vib–vii.

slave could without harm, that is, without guilt or punishment, desert his sacrilegious and heretic owner and go over to the Church, embrace the Catholic faith, and serve God in a more faithful way, which is nothing other than acquiring freedom by embracing the Catholic faith. This is what Accursius wanted to say in his brief gloss. And even if we were to concede to the opponent that neither the heretics nor the apostates of our time are included in that law and that even the slaves of the Manichaeans and Donatists obtain liberty by this law alone, he cannot deny that, notwithstanding the law of confiscation of the goods of the Manichaeans and Donatists, which was established by that law, the Christian slaves of those Manichaeans and Donatists obtain their freedom by virtue of the law *Deo nobis*, which was subsequently established by Justinian. In our time the same reasoning applies to Christian slaves who, notwithstanding the law of confiscation of the goods of heretics, acquire their freedom by virtue of the law *Deo nobis*.[21]

(6) As for the Canon Law by which we have confirmed our theory in the third place, he [the critic] responds that these laws apply only to the Christian slaves of those Jews who live in Christian lands and who have not received baptism, many of whom today live in Italy and many other Christian provinces. For this reason, he argues that [these laws] are implausibly extended to the Christian slaves of new Christians of Hebrew blood who nevertheless return to Judaism. In fact, they are not legally classified under the title of "Jews" but rather are included under the title of "heretics and apostates."

(7) The following has to be said about this: Although these laws explicitly speak only of slaves belonging to Jews who have not received baptism because in those places, where these decrees came to assist them, there were only those [Jews], and these laws were given to help stem their excesses. Nonetheless, equity requires us to suppose that those who made these laws did not intend that, if those [Jews] who were baptized and pretended to be Christians acquired Christian slaves, [these slaves] should be denied the privilege that they would enjoy in favor of the faith if their owners had not been baptized, especially because the baptism they received did not exclude their remaining true

---

21. Cod. 1.3.54.

Jews as they were before, nor did it diminish but rather increase the guilt of infidelity. All of these are punished in Spanish lands due to the crime of apostasy to [join] Judaism: they certainly derived their origin from those Jews who lived among Christians and who, pretending to be Christians, continued to live among themselves according to their rites. The law that applies to them was given by Gregory the Great who issued two epistolary decrees in the chapters *Mancipia* and *Fraternitatem*, distinction 54, and by Gregory IX who wrote the last chapter of the book *Extra De Iudeis et Saracenis*.[22] Following the civil laws and especially the law *Deo nobis*, these laws add a limitation: "When a slave has been bought for commercial purposes, etc.," and he wished him not to be harmed, as Gregory the Great shows sufficiently in the aforementioned chapter, *Mancipia*, in which he recalls these laws. Since these laws have been given by the emperors for the good of the faith and at the request of the Church, they have, in a certain sense, the force of Canon Law by the request and approval of the Church. It is also clear from this, as we have said above, that Christian slaves of apostates from the faith fall under the law *Deo nobis*. This can be confirmed thus: If there were no law handing the goods of the apostates to the treasury, no one would dare to say that the Christian slaves of apostates to Judaism are not covered by the Canon Law. Since the law of confiscation does not provide an exemption from the Canon Laws, which would apply even if [the law of confiscation] did not exist, the treasury cannot keep the goods of apostates from the faith beyond what belonged to them at the time of committing the crime; consequently, the quoted canons apply to the Christian slaves of those men who have fallen into Judaism.

(8) As for the last chapter taken from *De haereticis*, which in the fourth place confirms our theory, [the critic] replies that from the fact that in this chapter it is stated that those [slaves] who were evidently bound to a heretic are free from any bond of fidelity and any kind of obedience, it cannot be concluded that his slaves are to be freed. In this text it is judged that the debtors of a heretic are free from the obligation to repay the heretic, but they are not free [from paying their debts to] the treasury, which is the successor of the heretic's goods. Similarly, the

---

22. D. 54, chaps. 13 and 15.

vassals are free from compliance and obedience owed to him but not from compliance and obedience owed to the one who succeeds him according to that right. By the same token, although these slaves remain free from their owner by virtue of what has been said in that chapter, they no longer have the obligation to be at hand and to serve. They are, however, not thought to be free from the treasury, which is the successor of the heretic's goods. [The critic] confirms this [opinion] as valid, as he says, because the law that obliges the seizure of the goods of heretics without distinction had already been established under the same title by Innocence III in the chapter *Vergentis*. For this reason (although in that last chapter Gregory IX subsequently freed the slaves of a heretic owner), it does not follow that they become legally independent, since they had already been seized by the treasury by virtue of previous statutes, together with other goods of the same heretic.

(9) To this answer the following has to be said: Although the Christian slaves we are talking about do not strictly speaking become legally independent by virtue of that chapter nor are they freed from the power of the treasury (therefore non-Christians slaves, despite being freed from the bond with which they were tied to the heretic, are not free from the treasury), nonetheless, just as the children of heretics, since they are not tied to anyone but their father, by virtue of that chapter, are thought to be legally independent because their father committed heresy—as Alexander IV says in the chapter *Quicumque*, section *illorum, De haereticis*, book 6. For this reason, the usufruct of fortuitous goods they own does not belong to the treasury but to their children from the day their father committed the crime. Thus, the Christian slaves of these heretics obtained their freedom from the day their owner committed the crime, on the basis of the civil laws accepted and approved by the Church.[23] [Therefore] it has to be taken as certain that Gregory IX in that chapter intended to grant them that complete freedom (*absolutio*) that he could grant them according to the older laws. Hence, he made them legally independent from the day the owner committed his crime, and (as Alexander IV declared) the children of these heretics become legally independent in a similar fashion.

---

23. VI.5.2.2.

(10) To confirm this it must be said that, although the law of confiscation of goods [that transfers private goods to the public treasury] was established before the chapter *Vergentis* of Innocence III [was written],[24] it did not [establish that the goods] were to be rightfully made public on the day the crime was committed (this has been sanctioned after Gregory IX by Boniface VIII in the chapter *Cum secundum leges, de haereticis*, book 6) but at the time of sentencing.[25] For this reason, since the Christian slaves of heretics, according to the ancient laws and on the basis of Gregory IX, immediately become legally independent because of the crime of their owners, it follows, and the confirmation actually supports our view, that since the freedom of these slaves clearly precedes in time the right to a thing (*ius in re*), the treasury, according to the chapter *Vergentis*, acquires it [the right] only after the verdict. This law was not introduced to enrich the treasury but to punish and coerce the heretics, as Innocence III openly suggests in the chapter *Vergentis*.

(11) Last, it confirms [the critic's] point of view that even if we were to concede—he says—that according to Common Law the Christian slaves of heretics remain free, and because, after the tribunal of the holy Inquisition had been established in Portugal, such a law has been observed, one might believe that it was never accepted by us or that it was abrogated by the fact that custom dictated something to the contrary. Although their freedom does not prescribe over time, there is no reason why a freedom established by positive law may not prescribe, which in some cases establishes the freedom of a slave, because such prescription does not directly imply a violation of that freedom. As happens when a free man is captured to be a slave, he immediately loses the benefit granted by positive law by which a slave is made free and consequently it [the elimination of the positive law] only has the effect that he does not lose his servile condition [rather than introducing this condition].[26]

24. VI.5.2.1; Innocent's letter (*Vergentis*) is in VI.5.7.10.

25. *Made public* in this sense means "came to belong to the republic."

26. The argument is that the elimination of the positive right to freedom does not impose slavery on the captured but merely preserves the enslaved status that he already had, thus not directly destroying a right or freedom.

Since the rules of Common Law, which are the subject of this controversy, are not recent but rather very old, and since the Civil Law does not contradict the particular laws and customs of this kingdom, included in book 2 of the *Ordinationes*, title 5 by Portuguese king Manuel, I do not see what kind of plausibility there is in the argument that the Common Law, which we are here discussing, has never been accepted in this Portuguese kingdom.[27] And, if there is a contrary custom in this kingdom on this matter, it can only have begun at the time the tribunal of the Inquisition was established, because before that time it very rarely or never happened that the treasury had the chance to take the goods of heretics and apostates from the faith, especially [those goods] among which were slaves. And if such an opportunity presented itself at some point in time, it is uncertain whether they [the slaves] were granted their freedom. Although already forty years have now passed since the tribunal of the Inquisition was established in this kingdom, which is long enough to justify a prescription against the law, even regarding the Canon Law, it remains to be seen whether the doubts that have appeared in the meantime constitute an impediment for this prescription.

27. *Ordenações do reyno de Portugal*, lib. 2, tit. 5 at fol. vib–vii.

BIBLIOGRAPHY

Accursius. *Accursii Glossa in Digestum Vetus.* In *Corpus Glossatorum Juris Civilis,* edited by Mario Viola. Turin: Officina Erasmiana, 1969.

———. *Glossa in Codicem* in *Corpus Glossatorum Juris Civilis,* edited by Mario Viora. Turin: Officina Erasmiana, 1968.

Albornóz, Bartolomé de. *Arte de los contratos.* Valencia: Pedro de Huarte, 1573.

Aldama, J. A. "Luis de Molina S.J. De spe: Comentario a la 2a2ae, 17–22." *Archivo Teológico Granadino* 1 (1938): 111–48.

Alexandre, Salvador. *Judeus, Cristãos-novos e a inquisição.* Lisbon: Prefacio, 2002.

Almada, André Alvares de. *Tratado breve dos rios de Guine' do Cabo Verde.* Porto: Diogo Köpke/Typographia Commercial Portuense, 1841.

Andrade, Alonso de. *Varones ilustres de la Compañia de Iesus.* Madrid: Fernández de Buendía, 1666.

Angelus de Clavasio. *Summa de casibus conscientialibus, secunda pars.* Venice: Regazolae, 1578.

Añoveros, Jesús María García. "Carlos V y la abolición de la esclavitud de los indios: Causas, evolución y circunstancias." *Revista de Indias* 60 (2000): 58–84.

Antonino of Firenze. *Summa Theologica.* Verona: Typographia Seminarii apud Augustinum Crattonium,1740.

Azevedo, João Lúcio de. *Historia dos Cristãos Novos Portugueses.* Lisbon: Livraria Classica, 1922.

Azpilcueta, Martin de (Navarrus). *Enchiridion sive Manuale confessariorum et poenitentium.* Antwerp: Plantini, 1575.

———. *Enchiridion sive Manuale Confessariorum.* Rome: Ferrari, 1584.

Berger, Adolf. *Encyclopedic Dictionary of Roman Law.* Philadelphia: American Philosophical Society 1953.

Borucki, Alex, David Eltis, and David Wheat, "Atlantic History and the Slave Trade to Spanish America." *American Historical Review* 120 (2015): 433–61.

Buckland, Warwick. *The Roman Law of Slavery: The Condition of the Slave in Private Law from Augustus to Justinian.* Cambridge: Cambridge University Press, 1908.

Candido, Mariana P. *An African Slaving Port and the Atlantic World: Benguela and Its Hinterland.* Cambridge: Cambridge University Press, 2013.

"Carta de doação a Paulo Dias de Novais." In *Monumenta Missionaria Africana,* edited by António Brásio, 36–51. Vol. 3 of *África Occidental (1570–1599).* Lisbon: Agência Geral do Ultramar, 1953.

"Carta do Bispo de Cabo Verde a el Rey." In *Monumenta Missionaria Africana*, edited by António Brásio, 36–51. Vol. 3 of *África Occidental (1570–1599)*. Lisbon: Agência Geral do Ultramar, 1953.

Casares, Aurelia Martín. *La esclavitud en Granada en el siglo XVI*. Granada: Universidad de Granada, 2000.

Caspe, Luis de. *Cursus theologicus*. Lyon: Boissat and Anisson, 1643.

Castro, Alfonso de. *De iusta haereticorum punitione: libri tres*. Antwerp: Widow and Sons of Stelfius, 1568.

Chauhan, R. R. S. "Kunjali's Naval Challenge to the Portuguese." In *Essays in Goan History*, edited by Teotonio R. de Souza, 29–38. New Delhi: Concept, 2002.

Codex Iustinianus. Vol. 2 of *Corpus Iuris Civilis*, edited by Paul Krueger. Berlin: Weidmann, 1877.

Compilación de las Instrucciones del Oficio de la Santa Inquisición hechas por el muy Reverendo Señor Fray Tomás de Torquemada. Madrid: Diego Díaz de la Carrera, 1667.

Corpus Iuris Canonicis pars prior: Decretum Magistri Gratiani, edited by Emil Richter and Emil Friedberg. Graz: Druck and Verlagstanstalt, 1959.

Costello, Frank B. *The Political Philosophy of Luis de Molina, SJ (1535–1600)*. Rome/Spokane: Institutum historicum Societatis Iesu, 1974.

Covarrubias y Leyva, Diego. *In quartum decretalium librum epitome*. Lyon: Juntae, 1558.

———. *Regulae peccatum. De regulis iuris libro VI Relectio*. Venice: Rubinus, 1569.

———. *Variarum Resolutiones*. Frankfurt: Lechler, 1578.

Crone, G. R., trans. and ed. *The Voyages of Cadamosto and Other Documents on Western Africa in the Second Half of the Fifteenth Century*. London: Hakluyt Society, 1937. Reprint by Nendeln/Lichstentein: Kraus, 1967.

Cunha, Josephus Gerson da. *Contributions to the Study of Indo-Portuguese Numismatics*. Bombay: Education Society's Press, 1883.

Dari-Mattiacci, Giuseppe, and Guilherme de Oliveira, "Slavery versus Labor," *Review of Law & Economics* 17 (2021): 495–568.

dei Tudeschi Nicolò (Panormitanus). *Abbatis Panormitani in Quartum Quintum Decretalium*. Lyon: Fratres Senetonios, 1547.

———. *Commentaria super prima parte secundi libri decretalium*. Turin: Bevilaquae, 1577.

Diana, Antonino. *Coordinatus, seu Omnes resolutiones morales*. Lyon: Jean-Antoine Huguetan, 1680.

Disney, Anthony R. "Famine and Famine Relief in Portuguese India in the Sixteenth and Early Seventeenth Centuries," *Studia* 49 (1989): 255–81.

———. *The Portuguese in India and Other Studies, 1500–1700*. Routledge, 2018.

Eltis, David, and David Richardson, eds. *Atlas of the Transatlantic Slave Trade*. New Haven: Yale University Press, 2010.

Ercilla y Arteaga, Fortunio Garcia de. *Commentaria super titulo de justicia et iure* in *De ultimo fine juris canonici et civilis*. Bologna: Ruberiense, 1517.

Eymerich, Nicholas. *Directorium inquisitorum cum commentariis Francisci Pegnae*. Rome: Aedibus Populi Romani, 1587.

Fage, J. D. "Upper and Lower Guinea." In *The Cambridge History of Africa*, edited by J. D. Fage and Roland Oliver, 463–518. Vol. 3, *c. 1050–c. 1600*. Cambridge: Cambridge University Press, 1977.

Fagundez, Sebastião. *De iustitia et contractibus*. Lyon: Annison and Boissat, 1641.

Frier, Bruce W. *A Casebook on the Roman Law of Contracts*. Oxford: Oxford University Press, 2021.

García, Francisco. *Tratado utilísimo y muy general de todos los contratos*. Valencia: Ioan Navarro, 1583.

Hamann, Eike. *Die Begründung des Sklavenstatus bei den Postglossatoren: die Frage nach der Rezeption römischen Sklavenrechts*. Hamburg: Kovac, 2011.

Heimbach, Gustavus Ernestus, ed. *Authenticum: Novellarum Constitutionum Iustiniani*. Leipzig: Barth, 1851.

Heywood, Linda M. *Njinga of Angola, Africa's Warrior Queen*. Cambridge, Mass., and London: Harvard University Press, 2017.

Heywood, Linda M., and John K. Thornton, *Central Africans, Atlantic Creoles, and the Foundation of the Americas, 1585–1660*. Cambridge: Cambridge University Press, 2007.

Hurtado, Tomás. *Tractatus varii resolutionum moralium, pars posterior*. Lyon: Annison, 1651.

Jouvency, Joseph. *Historiæ Societatis Jesu pars quinta*. Rome: Plachi, 1710.

Justinian. *Institutiones. Digesta*. Vol. 1 of *Corpus Iuris Civilis*, edited by Paul Krueger and Theodor Mommsen. Berlin: Weidmann, 1889.

———. *Justinian's Institutes*. Translated with an introduction by Peter Birks and Grant McLeod. London: Duckworth, 2001.

Kaufmann, Matthias. "Slavery between Law, Morality, and Economy." In *A Companion to Luis de Molina*, edited by Matthias Kaufmann and Alexander Aichele, 183–225. Leiden/Boston: Brill, 2014.

Las Siete partidas del Sabio Rey don Alonso el nono, nuevamente glosadas por el Licenciado Gregorio López del Consejo Real de Indias de Su Magestad. Salamanca: Andrea de Portonaris, 1555.

Ledesma, Martin de. *Secunda quartae*. Coimbra: Juan Álvarez,1560.

Liber extravagantium decretalium (Liber extra). Vol. 2 of *Corpus iuris canonici*, edited by Emil Richter and Emil Friedberg. Leipzig: Bernhard Tauchnitz, 1881.

Liber sextus decretalium. Lyon, 1584.

Liber sextus decretalium. Vol. 2 of *Corpus iuris canonici*, edited by Emil Richter and Emil Friedberg. Leipzig: Bernhard Tauchnitz, 1881.

Litterae Annuae Societatis Iesu, Anni MDC. Antwerp: Nutio and Muerisio, 1618.

López, Luis. *De contractibus et negotiationibus*. Venice: Apud Iuntas, 1593.

Madrigal, Alfonso del (Tostado). *Commentaria in Primam partem Exodi*. Venice: Balleoniana, 1728.

Maffei, Giovanni Pietro. *Historiarum indicarum libri XVI*. Vienna: Trattneriana, 1752.

Maniscalco, Lorenzo. *Equity in Early Modern Legal Scholarship*. Leiden and Boston: Brill/Nijhoff, 2020.

Marcocci, Giuseppe. "Conscience and Empire: Politics and Moral Theology in the Early Modern Portuguese World." *Journal of Early Modern History* 18, no. 5 (2014): 473–94.

Mathew, K. S. "Calicut, the International Emporium of Maritime Trade and the Portuguese during the Sixteenth Century," *Proceedings of the Indian History Congress* 67 (2006–7): 251–70.

Mazzolini, Silvestro. *Summa Silvestrinae, pars secunda.* Venice: Dehuchini, 1587.

Mercado, Tomás de. *Tratos y contratos de mercaderes y tratantes.* Salamanca: Mathias Gast, 1569.

———. *Summa de tratos y contratos.* Sevilla: Fernando Díaz, 1587.

Miller, D. L. Carey. "Property." In *A Companion to Justinian's Institutes*, edited by Ernest Metzger, 42–79. London: Duckworth, 1997.

Mkenda, Festo. *Jesuits in Africa: A Historical Narrative from Ignatius of Loyola to Pedro Arrupe.* Leiden and Boston: Brill, 2022.

Molina, Luis de. *De iustitia et iure*, vol. 1. Cuenca: Ioannes Masselini, 1593.

———. *De iustitia et iure.* Venice: Sessa, 1611.

———. *De iustitia et iure.* Venice: Sessa, 1614.

———. *De iustitia et iure: Über die Gerechtigkeit und Recht.* Edited and translated by Matthias Kaufmann and Danaë Simmermacher and translated by Alexander Loose. Stuttgart/Bad Cannstatt: Frommann-Holzboog, 2019.

———. "Discurso Preliminar." In Vol. 1 of *Los seis libros de la justicia y el derecho*, translated and with a prologue and notes by Manuel Fraga Iribarne, 18–33. Madrid: Cosano, 1941.

Mota, Avelino Texeira da. *Brief Treatise on the Rivers of Guinea.* Translated by P. E. H. Hair and Jean Boulègue. Liverpool: University of Liverpool, 1984.

Mousinho, Manuel de Abreu. *Breve Discurso en que se cuenta la conquista del Reyno de Pegu.* Lisbon: Craesbeeck, 1617.

Navarra, Pedro de. *De ablatorum restitutione in foro conscientiae.* Toledo, Spain: Tomás Guzmán, 1597.

Ordenações do reyno de Portugal. Lisbon: Joam, 1565.

Palacio, Miguel de. *Praxis theologica de contractibus et restitutionibus.* Salamanca: Juan Fernández, 1585.

Peña, Francisco. *Flores commentariorum reverendissimi d. Francisci Pegnae in Directorium inquisitorum.* Milan: Bordonum, 1610.

Phillips, William D., Jr. *Slavery in Medieval and Early Modern Iberia.* Philadelphia: University of Pennsylvania Press, 2014.

Pinel, Ayres. *ad Constitutiones Cod. De Bonis Maternis.* Frankfurt: Bassaei, 1596.

Pinto, Paulo Jorge de Sousa. *The Portuguese and the Straits of Melaka, 1575–1619: Power, Trade and Diplomacy.* Singapore: NUS Press, 2012.

Quarta partida. Valladolid: Diego Férnandez de Córdoba, 1587.

Rabeneck, Iohannes. "De vita et scriptis Ludovicis Molina," *Archivum Historicum Societatis Iesu* 19 (1950): 75–145.

Rebello, Fernando. *Opus de obligationibus.* Lyon: Cardon, 1608.

Rio, Alice. *Slavery after Rome, 500–1100.* Oxford: Oxford University Press, 2017.

Rodney, Walter. "A Reconsideration of the Mane Invasions of Sierra Leone," *The Journal of African History*, 8 (1967): 219–46.

Russell-Wood, A. J. R. "Iberian Expansion and the Issue of Black Slavery:

Changing Portuguese Attitudes, 1440–1770," *American Historical Review* 83, no. 1 (1978): 16–42.

Salas, Juan de. "De contractu lusitanorum ementium aethiopes." In *De bello contra insulanos*, edited by Juan de la Peña, 14–18. Vol. 9 of *Corpus Hispanorum de Pace*. Madrid: C.S.I.C., 1982.

Sánchez, Tomás. *Consilia seu opuscula moralia.* Lyon: Prost, 1643.

Santos, João dos. *Ethiopia Oriental.* Evora: Manoel da Lira, 1609.

Schüßler, Rudolph. *The Debate on Probable Opinions in the Scholastic Tradition.* Leiden/Boston: Brill, 2019.

Schwartz, Daniel. *The Political Morality of the Late Scholastics: Civic Life, War and Conscience.* Cambridge: Cambridge University Press, 2019.

Scorraille, Raoul de. *François Suárez de la Compagnie de Jésus.* Paris: Lethielleux, 1914.

Simancas, Diego de. *De catholicis institutionibus.* Rome: Aedibus Populi Romani, 1575.

Simmermacher, Danaë. *Eigentum als ein subjektives Recht bei Luis de Molina (1535–1600). Dominium und Sklaverei in De Iustitia et Iure.* Berlin and Boston: de Gruyter, 2018.

Soto, Domingo de. *De la justicia y el derecho.* Translated by P. Marcelino Gonzáles Ordóñez. Madrid: Instituto de Estudios Políticos, 1967, with fascimile of *De iustitia et iure*, Salamanca: Portonariis, 1556.

Souza, Lúcio de. *The Portuguese Slave Trade in Early Modern Japan: Merchants, Jesuits and Japanese, Chinese, and Korean Slaves.* Leiden and Boston: Brill, 2019.

Stegmüller, Friedrich. *Geschichte des Molinismus.* Münster: Aschendorff, 1935.

Tellez, Balthazar. *Chronica da Companhia de Iesu nos Reynos Do Portugal.* Lisbon: Craesbeeck, 1647.

Tellkamp, Joerg Alejandro. "Rights and Dominium." In *A Companion to Luis de Molina*, edited by Matthias Kaufmann and Alexander Aichele, 125–53. Leiden and Boston: Brill, 2014.

Third Lateran Council. *Ita Quorundam.* In *Conciliorum Oecumenicorum Generaliumque Decreta*, edited by Giuseppe Alberigo and Antonio García y García. Turnhout: Brepols, 2013.

Thornton, John K. *Africa and Africans in the Making of the Atlantic World, 1400–1800.* Cambridge: Cambridge University Press, 1992.

———. *A History of West Central Africa to 1850.* Cambridge: Cambridge University Press, 2020.

Torquemada, Juan de. *In Gratiani decretorum, tomus primum.* Venice: Scoti, 1578.

Trullench, Egidio. *Operis moralis, tomus secundus.* Lyon: Anisson, 1652.

Turner, Cuthbert Hamilton. *Ecclesiae occidentalis monumenta iuris antiquissima: Concilia Gangrense et Antiochenum.* 2 vols. Oxford: Clarendon, 1913.

Vio, Thomas de (Cardinal Cajetan). *Commentaria in* Summa Theologiae. In Thomas Aquinas, *Opera omnia iussu impensaque Leonis XIII P. M. edita: Secunda secundae Summae theologiae; volume 9.* Rome: Typographia Polyglotta S. C. de Propaganda Fide, 1897.

Vitoria, Francisco de. "Letter to Bernardino Vique," in *Vitoria: Political Writings*, ed. Anthony Pagden and Jeremy Lawrance (Cambridge: Cambridge University Press, 1991).

Vives, José, ed. *Concilios visigóticos e hispano-romanos*. Barcelona and Madrid: CSIC and Instituto Enrique Flórez, 1963.

Vogt, John K. "The Lisbon Slave House and African Trade, 1486–1521," *Proceedings of the American Philosophical Society* 117 (1973): 1–16.

Wheat, David. *Atlantic Africa and the Spanish Caribbean, 1570–1640*. Williamsburg: University of North Carolina Press 2016.

Woltag, Johann-Christoph. "Postliminium." In *Max Planck Encyclopedias of International Law*. https://opil.ouplaw.com/display/10.1093/law:epil/9780199231690/law-9780199231690-e378.

INDEX

Also in the Early Modern Catholic Sources series

On the Moderation of Reason in Religious Matters
Lodovico Antonio Muratori
Translated by Ulrich L. Lehner

Jansenism: An International Anthology
Edited by Shaun Blanchard and Richard T. Yoder

Discourses on the State and Grandeurs of Jesus:
The Ineffable Union of the Deity with Humanity
Pierre De Bérulle
Translated by Lisa Richmond

A Defense of the Catholic Religion:
The Necessity, Existence, and Limits of an Infallible Church
Beda Mayr, OSB
Translated by Ulrich L. Lehner

Metaphysical Disputations III and IV:
On Being's Passions in General and Its Principles
and On Transcendental Unity in General
Francisco Suárez
Translated and annotated, with corrected Latin text,
by Shane Duarte